LIVING
WHAT YOU
BELIEVE

LIVING WHAT YOU BELIEVE

WISDOM FROM THE BOOK OF JAMES

KENNETH BOA & WILLIAM KRUIDENIER

NAVPRESS®

Bringing Truth to Life
P.O. Box 35001, Colorado Springs, Colorado 80935

Our Guarantee to You

We believe so strongly in the message of our books that we are making this quality guarantee to you. If for any reason you are disappointed with the content of this book, return the title page to us with your name and address and we will refund to you the list price of the book. To help us serve you better, please briefly describe why you were disappointed. Mail your refund request to: NavPress, P.O. Box 35002, Colorado Springs, CO 80935.

The Navigators is an international Christian organization. Our mission is to reach, disciple, and equip people to know Christ and to make Him known through successive generations. We envision multitudes of diverse people in the United States and every other nation who have a passionate love for Christ, live a lifestyle of sharing Christ's love, and multiply spiritual laborers among those without Christ.

NavPress is the publishing ministry of The Navigators. NavPress publications help believers learn biblical truth and apply what they learn to their lives and ministries. Our mission is to stimulate spiritual formation among our readers.

©2000 by Kenneth Boa and William Kruidenier
All rights reserved. No part of this publication may be reproduced in any form without written permission from NavPress, P.O. Box 35001, Colorado Springs, CO 80935.
www.navpress.com
Library of Congress Catalog Card Number: 00-055001

NAVPRESS, BRINGING TRUTH TO LIFE, and the NAVPRESS logo are registered trademarks of NavPress. Absence of ® in connection with marks of NavPress or other parties does not indicate an absence of registration of those marks.

ISBN 1-57683-198-1

Cover design by Dan Jamison
Cover photograph by Dale Wilson / Masterfile
Creative Team: Eric Stanford, Darla Hightower, Laura Spray

Some of the anecdotal illustrations in this book are true-to-life and are included with the permission of the persons involved. All other illustrations are composites of real situations, and any resemblance to people living or dead is coincidental.

Unless otherwise identified, all Scripture quotations in this publication are taken from the *New American Standard Bible* (nasb), Updated Edition © The Lockman Foundation 1960, 1962, 1963, 1968, 1971, 1972, 1973, 1975, 1977, 1995.

Library of Congress Cataloging-in-Publication Data
Boa, Kenneth.
     Living what you believe : wisdom from the book of James / Kenneth Boa & William Kruidenier.
          p. cm.
     ISBN 1-57683-198-1
     1. Bible. NT. James--Textbooks. 2. Christian life--Biblical teaching.
I. Kruidenier, William. II. Title.
  BS2785.5 B63 2000
  227'.91'0071--dc21   00-055001
Printed in the United States of America

2 3 4 5 6 7 8 9 10 / 08 07 06 05 04 03

FOR A FREE CATALOG OF
NAVPRESS BOOKS & BIBLE STUDIES,
CALL 1-800-366-7788 (USA)
OR 1-416-499-4615 (CANADA)

TABLE OF CONTENTS

Acknowledgments

The first time I, William, taught the book of James was a quarter-century ago in John and Mary Love Eysters' basement. A rookie teacher trying to hold the attention of squirming junior highers could have been a recipe for disaster, and might have been had the Eysters not prayed us through that summer. I have remained grateful since for their encouragement and the example of faith and works in their lives.

To the Spiritual Traveler

There are lots of ways to get from one place to another when you're traveling. A trip to a local bookstore will reveal a wide variety of resources, and the one you choose will probably be based on the kind of trip you are planning.

For instance, if you are driving to a nearby town, all you need is a fold-out road map, available at any convenience store or gas station. Millions of these soda-stained, misfolded, marked-up lifesavers fill the glove boxes of automobiles around the world. Road maps are the simplest set of instructions for getting from point A to point B. They contain no pictures, no historical anecdotes, no restaurant guides, no suggestions for entertainment or recreation. They simply tell you what you need to know: turn here, go there, stay on course. Patiently follow the squiggly red and blue lines and soon your destination appears miraculously through your windshield.

But what if you want to make a survey of a historically rich corner of your state, an area loaded with out-of-the way spots where you could spend an hour or a day? Not to worry: There are resources available for this kind of travel as well. They contain the instructions for how to get there (the road map part) and much more: side trips, photographs, drawings, guides for walking tours, and interviews with local residents. These guides are often written by natives who have grown up in the region and are passionate about it; and they want you to share their passion.

Then there are resources for people who like to do their traveling from the comfort and security of an easy chair, sitting in front of a crackling fire. With hot chocolate and a cookie or two, they settle in with an oversized pictorial panorama and spend an evening thumbing through the full-color pictures of their "destination." These trips-in-a-book are designed to stimulate the imagination and make you marvel at the possibilities that await your actual visit. Now you can also purchase video travelogues that replace a plane ticket with the TV remote—one click and you're on your way. And the Internet, with its digital destinations, is another story!

Road maps, area guides, and picture books are just a few examples of what's available to the geographical traveler. But what about the spiritual traveler, the person whose destination is Christlikeness via study of the Bible? The GUIDEBOOK you hold in your hands is written to help make your spiritual journey interesting, understandable, and enjoyable—and most of all, life-changing. While God has provided the basic road map, the Bible, you'll find the GUIDEBOOKS to be much like the travelers' guides that offer insights, side trips, vignettes, and pictures to illuminate and expand your understanding while on the way.

As you study the New Testament book of James, you'll discover some of the richest and most practical—and at times controversial—points that you will visit on your journey to Christlikeness. I pray that *Living What You Believe: Wisdom from the Book of James* will provide just what you need to make your journey a successful one. As a fellow traveler, let me encourage you to take all the side trips, work carefully through all the exercises, and avail yourself of every opportunity to make your journey through James a life-changing one. After all, the road to Christlikeness is the trip of a lifetime!

—Ken Boa

As You Study

The path to spiritual maturity is lined by many essentials. The indwelling presence of the Holy Spirit, the counsel and fellowship of other believers, disciplines and practices that lead to godliness, trials and tribulations—all make their distinct contributions to our growth. But perhaps most essential is the Spirit-led study of the Word of God. It is in the pages of the Bible that we learn of God's plan for the human race and develop a worldview—beliefs and practices—that will conform our life to His plan, ensuring our ultimate spiritual maturity.

The Bible becomes a taut line stretched between immaturity and maturity that keeps us from losing our way. The Bible introduces us to that great cloud of witnesses who have traversed the narrow way before us—stumbling, falling, getting up, and pressing on—helping us to see that others with clay feet have made it, and that we can too. And the Bible teaches, exposes, corrects, and trains us in that very thing toward which we are journeying: the righteousness of God made our own. Like a recipe for a prize-winning pie, every ingredient is essential. But there is a sense in which the Bible is the recipe itself—the *sine qua non* ("without which not," as the scholars like to say)—of the Christian experience.

The GUIDEBOOK series is designed to help you get the most out of the Bible. We have written this book because we, like you, are on the path toward maturity. If what we have learned along the way can encourage and help you—point out a beautiful view, offer an insight, or extend a helping hand over a rough spot in the road—then our goal will have been met. Because the paths of all Christian believers will converge at the gates of God's kingdom, we look forward to joining you there in that great day when Christ is revealed in us all.

—William Kruidenier

Getting the Most from Your Study

1. **Begin with prayer.** You can gain information on your own, but only God can reveal truth.
2. **Do not read commentaries on James until you have finished the entire study.** Self-discovery of biblical truth is exciting. It makes the Word of God come alive, and it also helps you retain what you've learned.
3. **Make sure you understand the structure of this GUIDEBOOK before you begin.** Explanations are found on page 9.
4. **Do not skip over directions to read the referenced Scriptures.** The text that follows may not make sense if you have not first read the Scripture passage(s).
5. **Be sure to write your answers to the study questions in the space provided.** Repetition and space for content interaction have been included to help you retain the material. Your answers will be confirmed in subsequent readings. These answers are intended to reinforce what you've already read and written.
6. **Work on this study every day of the week.** Begin the first day of your study week by reading the "unit introduction." Work through the Daily Excursions over the next five days. Then end your week with review and Scripture memory. You may want to preview "Sharing the Journey" if you are using this study with a group.
7. **Read the articles and suggested Daily Readings in the optional Side Tours, even if you don't have time to do the activities.** The articles and readings are important, and they can be read in a few minutes.
8. **During your day, meditate on what you've learned.** Most Daily Excursions can be completed in less than twenty minutes, but they are tightly packed. Reflecting on your observations allows biblical truths to expand your understanding and to take shape in your life.

HOW TO USE THIS GUIDEBOOK

INSTRUCTIONAL DESIGN©

GUIDEBOOKS are self-contained, interactive Bible studies. These studies are primarily inductive; that is, they lead the reader to related Scriptures throughout the Bible so that he or she might experience the joy of self-discovery as revealed by the Master Himself. Therefore, in addition to Scripture references from the key texts, topics are supported by the whole counsel of God. Other outside material and additional Scripture references are included in "For further study."

Each GUIDEBOOK includes five study units divided into five **Daily Excursions**. Most Excursions take about twenty minutes to complete. No additional reference materials are needed. To complete the optional Side Tours, a Bible and a concordance are sometimes needed.

PAGE DESCRIPTION

GUIDEBOOKS are designed for open, two-page viewing. Each page is divided into two columns—a wide inside column and a narrow outside column, as shown below. Daily Excursions include Bible teaching, related questions, life application (Bringing It Home), and Bible reading. The outside columns contain related Road Map and Side Tour options. At the end of each unit, it is suggested that the reader select one verse from the weekly reading to memorize.

The **Road Map** includes all Bible verses referred to in the Daily Excursions, except for lengthy study texts. (These are provided in appendix A.) Scriptures in the Road Map are linked to reference numbers in the Daily Excursions and numbered consecutively throughout the GUIDEBOOK. Unless otherwise noted, all Scripture passages are from the *New American Standard Bible,* Updated Edition.

Within quoted Scriptures, ellipses (. . .) indicate where portions of text have been omitted (due to space constraints) without compromising the meaning. The verses provided include the essential information for your study; however, you will benefit from reading the full text from your Bible.

The **Side Tours** contain optional reading and Scripture references related to Language & Literature, History & Culture, Bible Study Techniques, Cross References, Scripture Meditation, and Points of Interest (including life illustrations). All Side Tours are referenced in the text and numbered consecutively (preceded by "T") throughout the GUIDEBOOK. For example, the notation [T1] will follow the appropriate text in the Daily Excursion, and this same notation will appear in the adjacent Side Tour column. Because the Scriptures listed in Side Tours are not printed in this GUIDEBOOK, they must be looked up in a Bible.

Personal experiences of the authors are differentiated by their names in parentheses.

ROAD MAP	DAILY EXCURSION
	DAY 1
	EXAMINING PROVERBS AS LITERATURE
[1]PROVERBS 1 1 The proverbs [*mashal*] of Solomon the son of David, king of Israel; 2 To know wisdom and instruction, To discern the sayings of understanding, 3 To receive instruction in	What defines a proverb? The Hebrew word for "proverb" is transliterated[T1] *mashal*, which means "a discourse or a parable." *Mashal* comes from a root word that means "to be similar or parallel; to represent; to be like or be compared to." The book of Proverbs uses comparisons as

DAILY EXCURSION	SIDE TOURS
BRINGING IT HOME . . . 1. Look back at your life—as a child, a teen, and a young adult. Also look at your life now. At what point, if any, did you make a choice to reject being naive and foolish and to embrace wisdom? In what ways does that choice still impact your life today?	**HISTORY & CULTURE:[T3]** AUTHORSHIP—King Solomon, son of David, did not write all of the proverbs, but his work makes up the greater part of the book. Solomon was an observer and a seeker of knowledge. Not only was Solomon's knowledge encyclopedic, his understanding and discernment were such that his

INTRODUCTION — LIVING WHAT YOU BELIEVE

PROVERBS 1

20-33 Wisdom shouts in the street, she lifts her voice in the square; at the head of the noisy streets she cries out; at the entrance of the gates in the city, she utters her sayings: "How long, O naive ones, will you love being simple-minded? And scoffers delight themselves in scoffing and fools hate knowledge? Turn to my reproof, behold, I will pour out my spirit on you; I will make my words known to you. Because I called, and you refused; I stretched out my hand, and no one paid attention; and you neglected all my counsel and did not want my reproof; I will also laugh at your calamity; I will mock when your dread comes, when your dread comes like a storm and your calamity comes like a whirlwind, when distress and anguish come upon you. Then they will call on me, but I will not answer; they will seek me diligently but they will not find me, because they hated knowledge and did not choose the fear of the Lord. They would not accept my counsel, they spurned all my reproof. So they shall eat of the fruit of their own way and be satiated with their own devices. For the waywardness of the naive will kill them, and the complacency of fools will destroy them. But he who listens to me shall live securely and will be at ease from the dread of evil."

James' readers were among the "twelve tribes who are dispersed abroad" (James 1:1). The who? Answering that question will provide needed insight into the letter James wrote, the nature of what he said, and how we can profit from it today.

First, who was James? He was most likely the half brother of Jesus Christ (meaning he was the natural progeny of Joseph and Mary, born after Jesus). James was among the leaders of the fledgling church in Jerusalem that grew up after the ascension of Christ and the giving of the gift of the Holy Spirit (Acts 12:17; 15:13; 21:18; Galatians 2:9,12). James, then, was a Jewish convert to Christianity who was among the leaders of the predominantly Jewish church in Jerusalem.

And the "twelve tribes who are dispersed abroad"? They were Jewish converts to Christianity who had fled Jerusalem and its environs under threat of persecution from the Jews. James' letter was very possibly the first epistle written by an apostle to the early believers, most of whom were Jewish converts. As such, it reflects Old Testament characteristics. Like the Old Testament prophets, James was plainspoken about sin, emphasizing the necessity to live what you say you believe. Like the Old Testament wisdom books (specifically Proverbs), James focuses on living the spiritual life skillfully — being wise in the face of pressures to be otherwise. There is nothing theoretical and abstract about James; he is hands-on and concrete: "Don't tell me about your faith. Show it to me!" Paul's letters would later add the theological sophistication by which the Jewish-Gentile church developed. But in the pre-Pauline era, James used his hard-hitting, brother-of-a-carpenter Old Testament style to build up the early church. They would be together in belief and behavior if not in location.

Like James' readers, the church today has no central geographical base or home church. We are dispersed throughout the world, facing the daily challenges of remaining faithful in many areas of life: trials, temptations, relationships, speech, finances, good works, prayer, planning. All the while we are trying to remain humble before the Lord. *Living What You Believe: Wisdom from the Book of James* has the same goal as James' original "guidebook" did for first-century Christians: encouraging believers to validate their belief by their behavior.

INTRODUCTION TO UNIT 1
WISDOM IN TROUBLES AND TEMPTATION (JAMES 1)

Destination: To integrate the truth that God has promised to provide wisdom to handle the trials and temptations that confront us in life.

When an older member of my (William's) extended family was struck with a disabling physical condition, it fell to me to assume responsibility for her affairs when her husband died. While I had begun playing an assisting role in their lives during the husband's final months — coordinating legal and financial matters, looking after finances, hiring and managing in-home health care workers — I quickly became overwhelmed with the complexities of the situation after he died. Handling this type of situation long-distance (I lived in another state) required skills I did not possess. I remember asking God often for help — for wisdom and skill — in knowing how to meet this family member's needs.

That was more than a decade ago. Since then I have had to expand my skill set considerably in carrying out my responsibilities to this family member. Though she has continued to live, she exists in a totally disabled condition physically. While there are other family members to consult on important decisions, I have become responsible for her day-to-day welfare. Navigating the maze of medical and insurance details, overseeing her limited finances, looking out for the home where she still lives, managing the cadre of around-the-clock sitters who administer her medications — I now possess a measure of wisdom in an area of life with which I was totally unfamiliar a few years ago.

Job said, "Man is born for trouble, as sparks fly upward" (Job 5:7). While sometimes trouble has malevolent or pernicious sources, more often than not the troubles and trials we experience come simply from living in a fallen world. Things rust and break. We get sick. We have conflicts with others. We are reviled for our faith. There is too much month for our money. And because of all that, we get personally tired and discouraged and wonder how we can go on.

Jewish sages had a word for the remedy for life's trouble — *hokmah*. We translate this word as "wisdom," but its basic meaning is "skill." Wisdom, therefore, is the skill of living. It's the ability to face an obstacle and figure out how to go over, around, or through it. It's the ability to persevere without giving up. It's the ability to navigate the dangerous shoals without shipwrecking our faith. James was a man with Jewish roots, and he wanted you to know that "when you encounter various trials," you should "ask of God," who will give the skill (wisdom) to make it through. You may never be baptized in the fire of long-term caregiver as I was, but you have experienced (and will experience) serious trials and troubles for which you feel totally unskilled, totally unprepared. What should you do? Ask God for the skills (the wisdom) to meet the challenge.

James' emphasis on acquiring wisdom has led many to refer to his letter as the New Testament's version of the book of Proverbs. Unit 1 of this GUIDEBOOK will help you explore the first chapter of James and discover why asking God for skill in living is the best way to face life's troubles and temptations. Acquiring wisdom is crucial for the journey to Christlikeness— becoming like the one who was Himself "the wisdom of God" (1 Corinthians 1:24).

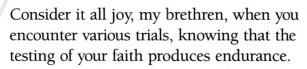

Consider it all joy, my brethren, when you
encounter various trials, knowing that the
testing of your faith produces endurance.

JAMES 1:2-3

DAY 1

OVERVIEW OF JAMES

JAMES AS LITERATURE

The book of James is a letter. And as such, it is not unique. Of the twenty-seven books of the New Testament, all but five (the four Gospels plus Acts) were letters in their original form.[T1]

AUTHOR, DATE, AND RECIPIENTS

Four different men named James are mentioned in the New Testament. Identify each one from the following verses:

- Matthew 10:2; Acts 12:2[1]

- Luke 6:16[2]

- Matthew 10:3; Acts 1:13[3]

- Matthew 13:55; Galatians 1:19[4]

Tradition has recognized the last of these four, James the half brother of Jesus, as the author of the letter. This James played a leading role in the first church council held in Jerusalem around AD 49–50 (Acts 15), and the letter produced by that council, under James' leadership, is similar in tone and style to the book of James. In particular, the same distinctive word for "greeting" is used in both the book of James (James 1:1) and the letter from the Jerusalem council (Acts 15:23)—and in no other apostolic letter in the New Testament.

The prominent disciple named James (in the inner circle of James, Peter, and John; see Matthew 17:1) was killed around AD 44, and neither of the other two Jameses occupies a prominent place in the New Testament. James the half brother of Jesus is the most reasonable choice as author of this letter.

Historians place the death of James at around AD 62–66, but evidence suggests his letter may have been written much earlier—as early as AD 46–49. If so, it was likely the first apostolic letter written to the early church (that is, the first letter that has been preserved). Several factors point to an early date of composition:

---

[1] MATTHEW 10; ACTS 12

Matthew 10:2 The names of the twelve apostles are these: The first, Simon, who is called Peter, and Andrew his brother; and James the son of Zebedee, and John his brother . . .

Acts 12:2 [Herod the king] had James the brother of John put to death with a sword.

[2] LUKE 6

16 . . . Judas the son of James . . .

[3] MATTHEW 10; ACTS 1

Matthew 10:3 . . . James the son of Alphaeus . . .

Acts 1:13 They went up to the upper room where they were staying; that is, Peter and John and James and Andrew, Philip and Thomas, Bartholomew and Matthew, James the son of Alphaeus, and Simon the Zealot, and Judas the son of James.

[4] MATTHEW 13; GALATIANS 1

Matthew 13:55 Is not His mother called Mary, and His brothers, James and Joseph and Simon and Judas?

Galatians 1:19 I did not see any other of the apostles except James, the Lord's brother.

[5] JAMES 1

1-3 James, a bond-servant of God and of the Lord Jesus Christ, to the twelve tribes who are dispersed abroad: Greetings. Consider it all joy, my brethren, when you encounter various trials, knowing that the testing of your faith produces endurance.

1. Jewish-Gentile relations, prominent in later New Testament letters (Romans and Galatians), are absent from this letter. That suggests a setting in which the church was still predominantly Jewish.

2. James' emphasis is on behavior rather than theology. The pattern in Paul's letters was often theology first, practice second (see, for example, Romans and Ephesians). This suggests an early period when faith was conceived of simply as belief in Jesus as the Jewish Messiah.

3. In the Greek text, James calls the meeting place of the church a "synagogue," an indication of the early, transitional setting for the letter (James 2:2). His references to church leadership also reflect a Jewish heritage, as he refers only to "teachers" and "elders" (James 3:1; 5:1).

4. James does not mention the watershed results of the Jerusalem council, which may indicate the letter was written before the council took place.

To whom did James address his letter (see James 1:1)?[5]

Where did they reside?[5]

According to James 1:2-3, what were they apparently experiencing?[5]

Most Bible scholars believe that "twelve tribes" were Jewish converts to Christianity who were driven out of Jerusalem in the persecution that arose after the martyrdom of Stephen.[T2]

Read the following verses and characterize the growth of the church in Jerusalem following the ascension of Christ:

- Acts 1:15[6]

- Acts 2:41[7]

- Acts 4:4[8]

- Acts 5:14[9]

- Acts 6:7[10]

When persecution began, where did the church flee (see Acts 8:1; 11:19)?[11]

LANGUAGE & LIT:[T1]

NEW TESTAMENT LETTERS— In addition to letters, the other distinct forms of literature in the New Testament are historical biography (the four Gospels), history (Acts), and apocalypse (Revelation, a letter written to seven churches in Asia Minor containing an apocalyptic vision given to John, the author, by Christ). While letters were normally addressed to individuals or certain groups, the "General Epistles" of the New Testament (James, 1 Peter, 2 Peter, 1-3 John, Jude) are so called because they were addressed to the church at large. The Old Testament makes occasional mention of letters (see 2 Samuel 11:14-15; 1 Kings 21:8-9; 2 Kings 5:5-7; 10:2-7; 19:14; Ezra 4:7-11; Nehemiah 2:8; 6:5), but none of the Old Testament books were written in that literary form.

The opening words of letters from this period of history followed a distinct pattern: "X (writer) to Y (recipient): Greetings (or a similar cordial greeting or blessing)." James follows this pattern precisely (see James 1:1), as do all the letters of the New Testament except Hebrews, 1 John, and Revelation. See Acts 15:23 and 23:26 for examples of other letters following this form.

HISTORY & CULTURE:[T2]

THE DIASPORA—When James referred to "the twelve tribes who are dispersed abroad," he used the Greek word *diaspora*, which means "scattered." The Diaspora, in modern terms, refers to the dispersion of Jews out of their homeland, beginning with the Assyrian and Babylonian captivities of the Old Testament. The presence of Jews in Gentile lands provided havens for the Jews driven out of Jerusalem who had become believers in Jesus the Messiah (Acts 8:1). Peter addressed his first letter to this same group (1 Peter 1:1; see also John 7:35).

How does this situation fit with James' words in James 1:2-3?[5]

THEME

The father of the Protestant Reformation, the great theologian Martin Luther, called James a "right strawy epistle." He, and others of his day, felt James' letter placed too much emphasis on works and not enough on faith. This view is understandable in that Luther and other Reformers were battling to reinstate faith to its rightful, biblical position after salvation by works had become a dominant emphasis in church teaching.

But James' letter is not contradictory to the letters of Paul ("the righteous man shall live by faith"; Romans 1:17); it is complementary to them. James stresses the truth that genuine faith will manifest itself in righteous living and that "faith, if it has no works, is dead" (James 2:17). The same criticisms leveled against James have been leveled against the teachings of Christ in the Sermon on the Mount, and understandably so—both stress the righteous lifestyle that should be evident among citizens of the kingdom of God.[T3]

The following two passages are perhaps the most central to James' message (for the verses, see appendix A). Summarize in your own words these primary themes of the letter.

- James 1:19-22

- James 2:14-17

---

[6]ACTS 1

15 Peter stood up in the midst of the brethren (a gathering of about one hundred and twenty persons was there together), and said . . .

[7]ACTS 2

41 Those who had received [Peter's] word were baptized; and that day there were added about three thousand souls.

[8]ACTS 4

4 Many of those who had heard the message believed; and the number of the men came to be about five thousand.

[9]ACTS 5

14 All the more believers in the Lord, multitudes of men and women, were constantly added to their number.

[10]ACTS 6

7 The word of God kept on spreading; and the number of the disciples continued to increase greatly in Jerusalem, and a great many of the priests were becoming obedient to the faith.

[11]ACTS 8; 11

8:1 On that day a great persecution began against the church in Jerusalem, and they were all scattered throughout the regions of Judea and Samaria, except the apostles.

11:19 Those who were scattered because of the persecution that occurred in connection with Stephen made their way to Phoenicia and Cyprus and Antioch.

[12]JAMES 1

5 If any of you lacks wisdom, let him ask of God, who gives to all generously and without reproach, and it will be given to him.

BRINGING IT HOME

1. What areas of life can you identify—whether spiritual, practical, relational, or moral—in which you need greater wisdom (skill)?

2. What do you see in James 1:5[12] that indicates God would welcome your request for increased wisdom in any area of your life?

3. Self-deception is subtle. Name any behavior in your life that is evidence of deception (James 1:22). What must you do not to be deceived any longer?

CROSS REFERENCES:[T3]

JESUS AND JAMES—To compare the influence of Jesus' teaching on His half brother's writing, compare the following verses in James with similar emphases in the Sermon on the Mount:

James	Matthew (Sermon on the Mount)
1:2	5:10-12
1:4	5:48
2:5	5:3
2:13	6:14-15
3:10-12	7:15-20
3:18	5:9
4:11	7:1-2
5:2-3	6:19-20
5:12	5:33-37

DAILY READING

Read Proverbs 2:1-8 (see appendix A) and underline all the action words associated with gaining wisdom and understanding from God.

DAY 2

THE OLD TESTAMENT ROOTS OF WISDOM

Wisdom is one of those words used by many and defined by few. We think we know wisdom when we see it, but we have a hard time telling anyone else how to look for it. While James encourages us to ask God for wisdom (James 1:5), if we discover the roots of wisdom in the Old Testament, we'll know better what we are asking for, how to know when we have received it, and how to make it a characteristic of our life.

THE SKILL OF WISDOM

As mentioned in the introduction, the Hebrew word for wisdom is *hokmah*, meaning "skill." This word, in its various forms (the verb "be wise," the adjective "wise," and the noun "wisdom"), occurs more than three hundred times in the Old Testament.[T4]

To see *hokmah* in its most practical, concrete settings, identify the "skill" that is referred to in each of the following verses:

- Exodus 28:3[13]

- Exodus 35:35[14]

- 2 Samuel 13:3[15]

- Psalm 58:5[16]

- Proverbs 30:24-28[17]

- Isaiah 40:20[18]

- Ezekiel 27:8[19]

Whether dexterity in engraving, shrewdness in negotiating, adroitness in navigating, passion in mourning, or discernment in speaking, skill was a valued characteristic in the Old Testament world. It is easy to see how the concept moved from the concrete realm of physical activity to the more abstract realm of words and ideas that today is most closely associated with *wisdom*. As examples of the more abstract expressions of wisdom in Hebrew thought, a wise person was one who was skilled in giving advice, interpreting dreams, settling disputes, or influencing and leading others.[T5]

THE ONLY WISE GOD

What does a wise person do? He or she, in a manner of speaking, brings order out of chaos. Take the building of the tabernacle, for instance. It took a group of wise (skilled) craftsmen to transform a multitude of raw resources—leathers, fabrics, metals, stones, and wood— into a beautiful worship center in the Sinai desert. Where did people learn such skills (that is, acquire such wisdom)? Because men and women are created in the image of God the Creator,[T6] they too can become skilled at bringing order out of chaos.

God is the One who, in the beginning, transformed a lifeless chaos (Genesis 1:2) into a living cosmos (Isaiah 42:5), and wisdom was His instrument of creation. Wisdom is personified in Proverbs 8, where it is pictured as being present with God in the creation of the world. Using Proverbs 8:22-31 (see appendix A), list the parts of the earth and universe to which God brought order by the use of wisdom.

God brought physical order out of chaos at Creation by employing His wisdom. He wants us, by the use of His wisdom, to bring order into the moral and spiritual chaos that sin has produced in the world—beginning with our own lives. Draw lines connecting the following verses with the area of life where wisdom brings order out of chaos:

• Proverbs 2:9-10[20]   The realm of personal peace

• Proverbs 2:12-15[21]   The realm of personal reputation

• Proverbs 2:16-17[22]   The realm of appropriate relationships

• Proverbs 3:4[23]   The realm of intellect and knowledge

• Proverbs 3:13,17[24]   The realm of sexual morality

STUDY TECHNIQUES:[T4]

WORD STUDIES—In ancient biblical Hebrew (unlike New Testament Greek), families of words are often centered around a common "tri-radical root." That's a fancy name for a root word consisting of three "radicals" (letters) that are all consonants. (Vowels were not written in ancient Hebrew, though they were pronounced. Signs indicating vowels were added to the consonants much later in the development of the language.)

The three consonants representing the word for "wisdom" were *h-k-m.* Adding the signs for the vowels eventually produced a family of "wisdom" words: *hakam* was the verb "be wise"; *hakām* was the adjective "wise"; and *hokmah* was the noun "wisdom." You can see the *h-k-m* root in each of these words.

The root of "wisdom" also appeared in some Hebrew names. A man named Hachmoni (or Hakmoni) was the father of Jehiel, who was the tutor of King David's sons (1 Chronicles 27:32). Another son of Hachmoni was one of David's mighty warriors, killing three hundred enemy soldiers with his spear at one time (1 Chronicles 11:11). Was Hachmoni the father of one son skilled in education and another in war? If so, finding the root of "wisdom" in his name (*h-k-m*) is not surprising.

A Bible study resource such as *Vine's Complete Expository Dictionary of Old and New Testament Words* will allow you to look up an English word such as *wisdom* and find discussions of the family of biblical words connected to it.

[20]**PROVERBS 2**

9-10 You will discern righteousness and justice and equity and every good course. For wisdom will enter your heart and knowledge will be pleasant to your soul.

[21]**PROVERBS 2**

12-15 To deliver you from the way of evil, from the man who speaks perverse things; from those who leave the paths of uprightness to walk in the ways of darkness; who delight in doing evil and rejoice in the perversity of evil; whose paths are crooked, and who are devious in their ways.

[22]**PROVERBS 2**

16-17 To deliver you from the strange woman, from the adulteress who flatters with her words; that leaves the companion of her youth and forgets the covenant of her God.

[23]**PROVERBS 3**

4 You will find favor and good repute in the sight of God and man.

[24]**PROVERBS 3**

13,17 How blessed is the man who finds wisdom and the man who gains understanding.

Her ways are pleasant ways and all her paths are peace.

[25]**PROVERBS 9**

10 The fear of the LORD is the beginning of wisdom, and the knowledge of the Holy One is understanding.

[26]**PROVERBS 8**

13 The fear of the LORD is to hate evil; pride and arrogance and the evil way and the perverted mouth, I hate.

WISDOM AND THE FEAR OF THE LORD

If wisdom belongs to God (Job 12:13; Daniel 2:20; Romans 16:27), how do we get it from Him? As mentioned previously, we have the potential for doing wise (skillful) things because we have been made in His image. But how do we know what is truly wise, and then how do we increase in wisdom?

One element in Scripture is consistently linked to the discovery and application of wisdom in life. To what is wisdom linked in Proverbs 9:10[25] (see also Job 28:28; Psalm 111:10; Proverbs 1:7; 15:33; Isaiah 33:6)?

In Psalm 34:11 the psalmist suggested that the fear of the Lord[T7] can be learned or acquired. How did the author of Proverbs suggest that one acquire (come to understand) the fear of the Lord? Summarize in your own words what you believe to be the theme of Proverbs 2:1-5 (found in appendix A).

JAMES AND THE OLD TESTAMENT ROOTS OF WISDOM

One verse in the Old Testament says what the fear of the Lord is: Proverbs 8:13.[26] Define the fear of the Lord based on this verse.

We can conclude the following about the Old Testament roots of wisdom:
- Abstaining from evil is to fear the Lord.
- To fear the Lord is to gain wisdom (skill in living).
- Therefore, abstaining from evil is to gain wisdom (skill in living).

James revealed his Old Testament understanding of wisdom by contrasting true wisdom with false wisdom. List the characteristics of each as found in James 3:13-18 (see appendix A):

True, Heavenly Wisdom	False, Earthly Wisdom

How does James' understanding of wisdom match that of the Old Testament?

BRINGING IT HOME

1. Obedience is at the heart of fearing God. Though James didn't per se mention the fear of the Lord in his letter, it is obvious that he wanted his readers to move beyond knowing God to obeying God. The letter you are about to study is filled with practical examples and exhortations to live in a manner that will cause you to gain wisdom. Perhaps now would be a good time to follow the admonition of Proverbs 2:3 ("Cry for discernment, lift your voice for understanding") and compose your own prayer, asking God for wisdom as you study James.

LANGUAGE & LIT:[T5]

AT THE HEART OF WISDOM— Acquiring wisdom takes diligence and discipline—doing what it takes to acquire the knowledge, practices, and perspectives that make one skillful.

What sets biblical wisdom apart from all other kinds (especially as seen in the book of Proverbs) is the desire to learn the skills for living according to God's principles and standards. Being biblically wise, therefore, is learning how to live in the kingdom of God as opposed to the realm of athletics, politics, or any other endeavor. While many verses in Proverbs seem unspiritual on the surface, they are designed to impart skills and wisdom that will bring success in the realm in which God is the judge.

CROSS REFERENCES:[T6]

LIKE FATHER, LIKE SON—All that humans are capable of doing reflects the image of God. We are able to become wise because God is wise, to love because God loves, to be creative because God is creative. We are even able to sin, not because God sins, but because God chooses—and God gave humans the ability to choose, even to choose between good and evil (Genesis 2:15-17; Joshua 24:15).

It is interesting to note that when Adam and Eve had their first child, Seth, the boy was said to have been created in the image of Adam, his father. Adam was made in the image of God (Genesis 5:1), Seth in the image of Adam (Genesis 5:3). The implication is that, while all human beings bear the image of God, we all also bear the sin-tarnished image of our forefather Adam.

DAILY READING

Read Proverbs 4 (see appendix A). Mark the benefits of wisdom you would like to acquire for your own life.

[27]**MATTHEW 4**
24 They brought to [Jesus] all who were ill, those suffering with various diseases and pains, demoniacs, epileptics, paralytics; and He healed them.

[28]**TITUS 3**
3 We also once were foolish ourselves, disobedient, deceived, enslaved to various lusts and pleasures, spending our life in malice and envy, hateful, hating one another.

[29]**HEBREWS 2**
4 God also testif[ied] . . . , both by signs and wonders and by various miracles and by gifts of the Holy Spirit according to His own will.

[30]**1 PETER 4**
10 As each one has received a special gift, employ it in serving one another as good stewards of the manifold grace of God.

[31]**JAMES 1**
4 And let endurance have its perfect result, so that you may be perfect and complete, lacking in nothing.

[32]**JAMES 1**
6-8 He must ask in faith without any doubting, for the one who doubts is like the surf of the sea, driven and tossed by the wind. For that man ought not to expect that he will receive anything from the Lord, being a double-minded man, unstable in all his ways.

DAY 3

HOW TO HANDLE TRIALS

You may not be in the same situation that James' readers were—scattered from your hometown, living in unfamiliar surroundings, not sure if you will ever see familiar faces again—but one thing connects you to them: trials! Suffering is a common thread that unites all humanity, but it takes on a special purpose for those who know God.

Before we discover James' insights on the "whys" and "hows" of trials, what is the largest trial looming on your horizon at the moment?

Keep that trial in mind as you study James' words, looking for insights and God's perspective on how you should handle it.

STEP ONE: PRAY FOR WISDOM

We are often tempted to think that the particular trial or stressful situation we are experiencing is too small or individualized for God's attention. James suggested otherwise when he referred to "various trials" (James 1:2). Before applying this phrase to your life, write down as many different trials as you can imagine that James' original audience might have been experiencing. (Remember, they had been uprooted from their homes in Jerusalem and scattered throughout Israel and the Roman provinces.)

The word for "many kinds"[T8] is used to describe other things in Scripture. Note how Scripture uses this same word in the following verses. (Look for the word "various" or the word "manifold.")

- Matthew 4:24[27]

- Titus 3:3[28]

- Hebrews 2:4[29]

- 1 Peter 4:10[30]

How do these examples help you understand the breadth of trials in your life?

One thing (among many!) that the non-Christian world finds strange about believers in Christ is our willingness to find joy in the midst of suffering. Why would anyone want to consider trials a joyful experience? James spelled it out clearly in verses 3[5] and 4.[31] Fill in the following phrases from these verses:

- Trials develop . . .

- Endurance develops . . .

Spiritually speaking, then, trials develop maturity in our lives, and for that reason are to be joyfully welcomed, not resisted. But there is also the practical matter of what to do in the midst of the trial. We can, after all, have a receptive attitude toward God's plan for our life without necessarily knowing how to carry it out or how to respond to the trial we are in. In that case, James said we should ask God for wisdom (James 1:5).

What specific kind of wisdom do you need in the trial you mentioned previously?

What condition did James say must be met in order to receive wisdom from the Lord?[32]

If we ask God in faith for resources to meet our family's needs, do we sit at home waiting for the resources to come, or do we go off to our job and work hard to earn those

POINT OF INTEREST:[T7]
FEAR OF THE LORD—It is understood that the fear of the Lord refers to awe, honor, submission, and respect. However, the Hebrew word for "fear" of the Lord is the same used for plain old fear—*yirah*. It is human nature that we honor those of whom we are ultimately afraid—afraid of their power to negatively affect our circumstances! Whether a wind-blown speeder in the presence of a policeman, or a guilt-ridden sinner in the hands of an angry God, a good dose of fear goes a long way toward producing awe and respect—and ultimately, wisdom.

STUDY TECHNIQUES:[T8]
WORD USAGE COMPARISON—The Greek word translated "many kinds" is *poikilos*. A helpful occurrence of this term is in the Septuagint (the Greek translation of the Old Testament) in Genesis 37:3. There it is used to describe the coat that Jacob made for his son Joseph. This famous "coat of many colors" serves as an object lesson for the trials of the believer. To the same infinite degree that one shade of color might vary from another in a hand-dyed, rainbow-hued garment, so is the potential variety of the trials facing the believer. Fortunately, our infinite God is capable of providing infinite wisdom for the unique needs of His children.

POINT OF INTEREST:[T9]
ACTING IN FAITH—In the early weeks of the new church, the twelve apostles were distracted from their main priorities: prayer and the ministry of the Word of God (Acts 6:2,4). What was the "ministry of the Word" at the time that the New Testament didn't exist? Apparently it was what they had been doing in Acts 1–5: preaching, baptizing, teaching, healing, being persecuted, overseeing the affairs of the church.
For the apostles, ministry was action. Like the apostles, we are to pray and then act, trusting God to meet us in our work for Him.

[33]JAMES 1

[33]**JAMES 1**

9-11 The brother of humble circumstances is to glory in his high position; and the rich man is to glory in his humiliation, because like flowering grass he will pass away. For the sun rises with a scorching wind and withers the grass; and its flower falls off and the beauty of its appearance is destroyed; so too the rich man in the midst of his pursuits will fade away.

[34]**JAMES 4**

6 [God] gives a greater grace. Therefore it says, "GOD IS OPPOSED TO THE PROUD, BUT GIVES GRACE TO THE HUMBLE."

[35]**JAMES 1**

12 Blessed is a man who perseveres under trial; for once he has been approved, he will receive the crown of life which the Lord has promised to those who love Him.

resources? Hopefully, we do the latter. Our part is to pray (ask in faith) and believe God (act in faith),[T9] trusting that in the midst of our actions He will make His answers and wisdom known to us.

STEP TWO: TAKE PRIDE IN YOUR POSITION

In light of the truth that sinful pride is at the root of all rebellion against God,[T10] James catches our attention by saying that we should "glory in [that is, 'be proud of'] our high position."[33] Remember, he was originally talking to a dispossessed and dispersed people who were perhaps at the lowest point in their lives. What was he saying? How could trials and troubles be a cause for boasting, pride, or glory?

James cast his discussion in terms of the rich (the self-sufficient) and the poor (the dependent). James was making no statements here on the value of wealth over poverty, nor vice versa. He was talking about a "low position" versus a "high position" in life,[33] and how God loves to come to the aid of the needy, those who need wisdom and help in their time of trial.

Using James 4:6[34] as your guide, write in your own words why those in need (those who permanently or temporarily find themselves in a low or humble place in life) should take pride in their position.

STEP THREE: PREPARE TO RECEIVE A CROWN

Spiritual myopia is a common affliction among Christians. Myopia in the medical world is nearsightedness—the inability to focus on distant objects. Spiritual myopia is the inability to focus on the ultimate spiritual destiny of the believer and use it as a backdrop for present realities. The need to focus on the future is particularly important when we are undergoing trials.

James gave a final reason for enduring, or persevering in (being joyful in), our trials.[35] What blessing[T11] is promised to the one who perseveres (endures)[5, 31, 35] and is approved?

BRINGING IT HOME

1. Write out the prayer for wisdom that you will present (or have been presenting) to God concerning the trial you are in:

2. Having asked in faith, what *acts* of faith can you take as a way to stay focused on believing God for His wisdom in your situation?

3. What ultimate goal should you have regardless of how long your present trial continues (James 1:12)?[35]

STUDY TECHNIQUES:[T10]

CROSS REFERENCES—Pride as a matter of boasting is not condemned in Scripture. The question is, in whom or what does one boast? When one boasts of, or is proud of, another (for example, a friend or God), pride is warranted. When one boasts in oneself, that boasting can become sinful and arrogant. Paul warned young men against conceit, the same sin by which Satan fell (1 Timothy 3:6).

For further study:
Sinful examples of pride: Leviticus 26:19; 2 Chronicles 26:16; Proverbs 13:10; 16:18; Isaiah 25:11; Jeremiah 13:9; 49:16; Daniel 5:20; Amos 6:8; Obadiah 3
Legitimate expressions of pride: 2 Corinthians 5:12; 7:4; 8:24

LANGUAGE & LIT:[T11]

BLESSEDNESS—Another indication of James' heritage as a Jewish believer is his use of "Blessed is . . ." (James 1:12). This was a classic phrase of blessing, bestowing the favor of the Lord, in Jewish literature (see Psalm 1:1 and fifteen other occurrences in Psalms). Outside of its famous use as a prefix to happiness in Jesus' Beatitudes (Matthew 5:3-12), James is the only other New Testament writer to use the phrase in the Old Testament sense of blessedness in suffering (compare John's "blessing" for reading the words of the revelation in Revelation 1:3).

DAILY READING

Read 2 Corinthians 6:3-10 and 11:23-33 (see appendix A) and note the number of trials in which Paul probably sought wisdom from God.

DAY 4

UNDERSTANDING TEMPTATIONS

[36]JAMES 1

13 Let no one say when he is tempted, "I am being tempted by God"; for God cannot be tempted by evil, and He Himself does not tempt anyone.

[37]JAMES 1

14 Each one is tempted when he is carried away and enticed by his own lust.

Let's face it: Trials often lead to temptations. On a tour of a snack food company's factory, the young daughter of a friend of mine (William) couldn't take the tedium any longer. As we stood next to a conveyor belt that dumped fresh-baked pretzels into empty plastic bags, the tempted tyke reached out, grabbed a fresh pretzel, and took a big bite—and tossed the remainder back onto the conveyor belt! Within moments, that personalized portion of the conveyor's cargo was sealed in a bag, destined for a shopper's grocery cart.

What made the littlest member of the tour yield when the older members (who were feeling the same temptation) resisted? She was tired, hungry, and bored—a tour of a factory is certainly a trial for a child. For her, the trial led to the temptation. And often our adult-sized trials lead to temptations as well. James is going to tell us why we sometimes give in.

WHAT GOD DOES NOT DO

The main reason that trials often become temptations is because they are, grammatically at least, the same thing. Look at a comparison of James 1:2[5] and 1:13[36]:

verse 2: Consider it all joy . . . when you encounter various trials [peirasmos].

verse 13: Let no one say when he is tempted [peirazo] . . .

In these verses, both "trials" and "tempted" are from the same primitive root word in Greek, peira, which means a trial or experiment.[T12] One is a verb form ("tempted"); the other is a noun ("trials"). Therefore, we could render verse 13 with a new word, "trialed": "Let no one say when he is trialed, 'I am being "trialed" by God'; for God cannot be trialed by evil, and He Himself does not trial anyone."

Not only are trials and temptations similar grammatically, but practically speaking they are similar as well. That is, when we are enduring a trial, there is always a temptation for us to find a way of escape that God has not provided. Therefore, a trial almost inevitably leads to a temptation.[T13] Take the Jews to whom James was writing— what might they have been tempted to do in light of the trials they were experiencing? (Remember, they were probably poor, with limited resources, far from home, persecuted, and discouraged.)

What about the personal trial that you noted in day 3? What temptations does that particular trial present to you?

James wanted his readers to understand that, though trials are allowed by God,[T14] God does not tempt us to sin by allowing us to endure trials.[5, 36] Review James 1:3-4 and write a reminder of why God allows our faith to be tested.[5, 31]

If temptation doesn't come from the external situation we're in, where does it come from? Read verse 14 and write down the source of our temptations.[37]

From the following two statements, circle the one best illustrating the truth that James was presenting:

1. "I am really tempted by that conveyor belt of pretzels."

2. "I am really tempted by my flesh (disposition to sin) to grab a pretzel."

Hopefully, you circled number two (see 1 John 1:8). There is nothing sinful about pretzels, money, position in life, appearance, or material objects. These things have no moral power, no will of their own, by which they can tempt or entice us. Rather, we are tempted by our self-willed nature, the lusts of our flesh, to violate existing standards of thought, word, or deed.

THE PATHOLOGY OF SIN

Pathology is the study of the causes, development, and consequences of disease. If we substitute the word "sin" for

CROSS REFERENCES:[T12]
THE ROOT OF TRIALS—The root word *peira* occurs only twice in the New Testament, both times in Hebrews (Hebrews 11:29,36). Helpfully, one use refers to an experiment (when the Egyptians tried to follow the Israelites through the Red Sea), and the other to painful trials endured by saints of old. In the latter use, the word is not translated in the English of modern versions. The Greek literally reads: "and others received a trial of mockings and scourgings."

CROSS REFERENCES:[T13]
THE WAY OF ESCAPE—A key illustration of the "who" and "how" of temptations is the account of Jesus in the wilderness (Matthew 4:1-11; Luke 4:1-13). God the Spirit led Jesus into the wilderness "to be tempted [*peirazo*] by the devil." It is clear in this instance that God led Jesus into a situation where His moral will would be tested, but God did not do the tempting. Rather, Satan did (compare 1 Corinthians 7:5). In that test the Devil offered Jesus three opportunities to escape, but He refused each one, preferring rather the approval of God over the approval of the Devil (compare Galatians 1:10).

Jesus' situation was an exact parallel to that of the first Adam in the Garden of Eden, who was similarly tested but who yielded, throwing himself and his descendants into sin (Genesis 3:1-19). Jesus' resistance to temptation won back the approval of God that Adam had lost.

A key passage on escaping temptation is 1 Corinthians 10:13, where believers are promised that God will *always* provide a way of escape. The implication is that believers are never forced to sin regardless of the strength of the temptation. There is always a way out of it.

³⁸JAMES 1

15 When lust has conceived, it gives birth to sin; and when sin is accomplished, it brings forth death.

³⁹PSALM 139

23-24 Search me, O God, and know my heart; try me and know my anxious thoughts; and see if there be any hurtful way in me, and lead me in the everlasting way.

⁴⁰JAMES 1

17 Every good thing given and every perfect gift is from above, coming down from the Father of lights, with whom there is no variation or shifting shadow.

⁴¹1 CORINTHIANS 10

13 No temptation has overtaken you but such as is common to man; and God is faithful, who will not allow you to be tempted beyond what you are able, but with the temptation will provide the way of escape also, so that you will be able to endure it.

"disease," we will discover a pathology of sin in James 1:15.[38] Fill in the following "pathology chart":[T15]

CAUSE: The conception of

DEVELOPMENT: The birth of

CONSEQUENCE: The resulting

Based on this pathology, it becomes clear that if we allow lust and desire to conceive within us, the resulting consequence will be spiritual death. Therefore, if we consider our ability to choose as a spiritual muscle, what beneficial role do tests and trials play in our lives?

How does this help us to understand the admonition to view trials with joy?[5, 35]

WHAT GOD DOES DO

There is a distinct possibility that, when undergoing trials, we may miss who God is and what He is doing. We may be so caught up in the pressures we are facing that we become deceived, blaming God for our temptation and even our sin. And here is the troubling fact: It's hard for deceived people to know they are deceived. How could Psalm 139:23-24 protect us from deception during a time of testing?[39]

James 1:17 tells us three things about God:[40]

1. He gives good things and perfect gifts. What does this tell you about the possibility of Him being the source of temptation?

2. He is the Father of lights (that is, the Creator of the sun and moon and stars). How do these heavenly bodies alter the appearance of things on earth?

3. He is always the same. Unlike appearances changed by shadows and light, God never changes. What comfort does this provide you regarding tests and trials?

BRINGING IT HOME

1. What would you tell a married friend who said the following: "If God didn't want me to fall in love with her, why did He bring us together at work"?

2. Write a short definition of "trials" and "temptations" based on what you have learned so far:

   Trials are . . .

   Temptations are . . .

3. The next time you are tempted to sin, what will be your focus?

CROSS REFERENCES:[T14]

THE PURPOSE OF TESTING—Some of the clearest references to testing in the Bible come from the early days of Israel's national relationship with the God who had plucked them out of slavery in Egypt. The instructions about gathering manna to eat were a test to see "whether or not they will walk in My instruction" (Exodus 16:4). The giving of the Ten Commandments amid the power and might of God was "to test you, and in order that the fear of Him may remain with you, so that you may not sin" (Exodus 20:20). Finally, the forty years of wandering in the wilderness was "that He might humble you, testing you, to know what was in your heart, whether you would keep His commandments or not" (Deuteronomy 8:2). God tests us to confirm our willingness not to sin; He never tempts us to sin.

POINT OF INTEREST:[T15]

NOTHING NEW UNDER THE SUN—The pathology of sin has not increased in sophistication even though the sins of humankind have. Lust (desire), leading to sin, leading to spiritual death, is what caused the sins of Eve (Genesis 3:6-22) and David, the king of Israel (2 Samuel 11:2-17). The apostle John captured the universality of lust and desire in 1 John 2:16: We sin through what we want, what we see, and who we want to be.

DAILY READING

Read 1 Corinthians 10:13[41] and try to identify the way of escape God is providing in any current trial you are facing (including simply enduring it until it is over!).

[42]**JAMES 1**
19-20 Everyone must be quick to hear, slow to speak and slow to anger; for the anger of man does not achieve the righteousness of God.

[43]**JAMES 1**
21 Putting aside all filthiness and all that remains of wickedness, in humility receive the word implanted, which is able to save your souls.

[44]**ISAIAH 55**
10-11 As the rain and the snow come down from heaven, and do not return there without watering the earth and making it bear and sprout, and furnishing seed to the sower and bread to the eater; so will My word be which goes forth from My mouth; it will not return to Me empty, without accomplishing what I desire, and without succeeding in the matter for which I sent it.

[45]**HEBREWS 4**
12 The word of God is living and active and sharper than any two-edged sword, and piercing as far as the division of soul and spirit, of both joints and marrow, and able to judge the thoughts and intentions of the heart.

[46]**2 TIMOTHY 3**
16 All Scripture is inspired by God and profitable for teaching, for reproof, for correction, for training in righteousness.

DAY 5

BECOMING REAL RELIGIOUS

We often encounter "tough on the outside, gentle on the inside" people who instill confidence by their servant leadership. James was that kind of person. Fifteen times in his letter he lovingly referred to his readers as "brethren" while at the same time laying down no-frills principles for kingdom living. James was a lot like his half brother, Jesus, in that he was not afraid to be real religious. He understood the true meaning of the word "religious."

HOW TO BE RIGHTEOUS

Literature and movies (and perhaps real life) sometimes present a distraught character at the end of her rope crying out, "God, what do You want from me?!" A good question, James would say, with a simple answer: a righteous life.[42] What James did not want for his beloved brethren[T16] was that they would become like the unrighteous people they had been thrown into the midst of in their dispersion from Jerusalem. The farther they got away from their home city and church, the deeper into pagan territory they went. Many were encountering personalities and practices they had never seen before.

And isn't that the way it is for us? Instead of being driven into the world by our persecutors, we have been sent into the world by our Lord—to represent Him to all nations (Matthew 28:18-20).[T17] Therefore, we must be righteous as He is righteous (1 John 3:7). Write in your own words James' summary statement about what short-circuits the righteousness God desires for us:[42]

James listed three things that characterize a person who is intent on manifesting the righteousness of God. What are they?[42, T18]

1.

2.

3.

James next said how to be righteous, and he did so in negative terms as well as positive terms. What are we to reject?[43]

What are we to accept?[43]

Not only were we brought to God by the word of truth, but also we are to manifest righteousness by bearing the fruit of the word. "In the exercise of His will He brought us forth by the word of truth, so that we would be a kind of first fruits among His creatures" (James 1:18). James' image of the Word of God as a seed "implanted" is a beautiful one.[43] What is the ultimate purpose of a seed planted in the ground?[T19]

HOW TO BE BLESSED

If we are to manifest righteousness by allowing the Word to bear fruit through us, how do we do that? And what are the results? And how are we to understand this concept of the Bible being "alive"—like a seed that brings forth fruit?

Record your observations on how the Word of God can change us through its "aliveness":

- Isaiah 55:10-11[44]

- Hebrews 4:12[45]

- 2 Timothy 3:16[46]

Most people would not rank looking in a mirror very high on their list of blessings! And that is exactly James' point. He said, "If anyone is a hearer of the word and not a doer, he is like a man who looks at his natural face in a

CROSS REFERENCES:[T16]

BELOVED BRETHREN—James referred to his readers as his "brethren" fifteen times (1:2,16,19; 2:1,5,14; 3:1,10,12; 4:11; 5:7, 9-10,12,19). Three of the fifteen times he even referred to them as "beloved brethren" (1:16,19; 2:5). This display of James' abundance of affection for his readers is surpassed in the New Testament only by Paul in 1 Corinthians (twenty-seven occurrences of "brethren") and 1 Thessalonians (eighteen occurrences). Interestingly, the letter with the most correctives of any New Testament letter, 1 Corinthians, is the one where Paul referred to the errant church as his brothers most often. That tells us something about the need for affection in correction.

POINT OF INTEREST:[T17]

AMBASSADORS—Even though a case could be argued that only Paul and the apostles were ambassadors, based on the two instances of the word in 2 Corinthians 5:20 and Ephesians 6:20, most feel that the role of ambassador applies to every Christian as we represent Christ in the world to others—the chief job of an ambassador. But it is easy to see that righteousness befits an ambassador, since the word for being an ambassador is *presbeuo*, the verb form of *presbuteros*, the word for "elder." Paul certainly outlined the godly character of an elder in clear enough terms (1 Timothy 3:1-7; Titus 1:6-9). Therefore, there can be little doubt that righteousness befits the role of those who represent Christ in the world.

47 JAMES 1

25 One who looks intently at the perfect law, the law of liberty, and abides by it, not having become a forgetful hearer but an effectual doer, this man will be blessed in what he does.

48 JAMES 1

26 If anyone thinks himself to be religious, and yet does not bridle his tongue but deceives his own heart, this man's religion is worthless.

49 MARK 7

20-23 [Jesus] was saying, "That which proceeds out of the man, that is what defiles the man. For from within, out of the heart of men, proceed the evil thoughts, fornications, thefts, murders, adulteries, deeds of coveting and wickedness, as well as deceit, sensuality, envy, slander, pride and foolishness. All these evil things proceed from within and defile the man."

50 JAMES 1

27 Pure and undefiled religion in the sight of our God and Father is this: to visit orphans and widows in their distress, and to keep oneself unstained by the world.

51 MARK 12

38-40 In His teaching [Jesus] was saying: "Beware of the scribes who like to walk around in long robes, and like respectful greetings in the market places, and chief seats in the synagogues and places of honor at banquets, who devour widows' houses, and for appearance's sake offer long prayers; these will receive greater condemnation."

mirror; for once he has looked at himself and gone away, he has immediately forgotten what kind of person he was (James 1:23-24). Looking in a mirror and seeing our own (un)righteousness is sort of like the blind leading the blind. But when we look "intently at the perfect law," we see freedom. What did James mean by "freedom"?[47]

What is the condition for experiencing that freedom?[48]

HOW TO BE REAL RELIGIOUS

Religion has taken more than its fair share of criticism through the centuries. But James was not one of its naysayers. He believed in being religious—as long as your religion is real! Don't forget, James was speaking out of a background of tremendous religious hypocrisy in Israel. The prophets of the Old Testament had railed against Jewish priests and leaders for being religious on the outside but defiled on the inside. More specifically, James knew that Jesus had sharply disagreed with the Pharisees about the nature of true religious expression.

James wanted to emphasize to his believing fellow Jews that the days of Pharisaism were over. No longer was it acceptable to be "clean" on the outside and "dirty" on the inside. Eventually, what is on the inside will come out and reveal whether a person is truly religious or not. James used speech as an example of what can negate a person's religious testimony. How do his words compare to Jesus' words in Mark 7:20-23?[49]

Why did James use looking after orphans and widows as an example of true religion?[50]

How does looking after the needy compare with being a public, recognized, adulated religious leader?

If a person claims to be religious but is "spotted by" (shares the same moral standards as) the world, what is his or her religion worth?[48]

BRINGING IT HOME

1. A modern clothing manufacturer has popularized the slogan "Just do it!" James would have liked that direct approach. But instead of using a mirror to check our clothing, he would recommend using the mirror of the Bible to check our life. Which mirror do you think is getting the most attention from Christians today? Why?

2. How about your life? What have you been seeing in recent days as you have looked into the mirror of God's Word? What are you learning about the value of your religion?

3. In our "afraid to offend" culture, how are you reacting to James—a leader who was willing to speak plainly about the value of one's religion?

LANGUAGE & LIT:[T18]

PLUTARCH SAYS—The Greek biographer and philosopher Plutarch (about AD 46–120) wrote that "nature has given to each of us two ears and one tongue, because we ought to do less talking than listening." Not bad advice, though without counting body parts, we could deduce the same thing from Proverbs 12:16; 17:27-28; 18:13; and 29:20.

HISTORY & CULTURE:[T19]

BEARING FRUIT—The agricultural environment of the first century AD gave rise to picturesque metaphors for describing the spiritual life. One of the most helpful is that of fruit bearing. Jesus not only used this metaphor in His teachings (Matthew 7:17-19; 12:33; 21:43) and His parables (Matthew 13:1-23), but Paul used it to refer to maturity in Christian living and in ministry (Romans 1:13; 7:4; 15:28; Galatians 5:22-23; Ephesians 5:9; Colossians 1:6,10). It is interesting to speculate on what might be used today, in our technological world, as a metaphor for maturity.

DAILY READING

Read Mark 12:38-40.[51] Mark any verses that violate James' teaching about true religion.

To the leader: As an option, you may wish to seal the group members' written prayers for wisdom in separate envelopes with their names on them, so that you can give these back to their owners at the end of the study and let them see how God has answered their prayers.

1. The book of James is a letter written by a half brother of Jesus to Jewish Christians who had been driven out of their homeland by persecution. It stresses the truth that genuine faith manifests itself in righteous living.
   - How well would you say you already know the book of James? What are you hoping to get out of this study of the book?
   - What were the life situations of the writer and of his original readers? Given that background, what should we be looking out for as we proceed in our study of the letter?
   - Read aloud your summary of the primary themes in the book of James. How is your summary different from that of others in the group? How is it the same?

2. In the Old Testament sense, wisdom is skill in living. Fundamentally, it involves being obedient to God.
   - What would the people closest to you identify as your top skills? Just for fun, demonstrate one of your more frivolous skills to the group—making a bird out of folded paper, patting your head with one hand while rubbing your tummy with the other, whatever.
   - Life at Minnie's house has been getting more and more out of control. Her three teenage children come and go at different times. Messages don't always get communicated and chores don't always get done. There's noise. There's mess. Minnie's ready to make some changes. What are some ways that Minnie could use her wisdom to bring order out of the chaos in her home?

   - Do you obey God because you are wise, or do you become wise by obeying God? Explain your reasoning.

3. James' readers were undergoing suffering, and so James pointed to some of the good things that can result from trials.
   - As you look back, what examples from your own Christian life prove James' contention that tests of faith build endurance, leading to spiritual maturity?
   - Think of one specific test of your faith that you went through in the past. What kinds of wisdom did you need for that test? Is it your natural reaction, when a trial comes upon you, to ask God for wisdom to deal with it, believing implicitly that He will give it? If not, why not?
   - Not many of us are imprisoned or put to death for our faith, as the early Christians were. But in what other ways might it be our privilege to suffer for Christ?
   - (1) Christians are too focused on "pie in the sky," too heavenly minded to be of much earthly good. (2) Christians are too quick to demand God give them blessings in this life, not satisfied with God's promises of reward in the afterlife. Which statement (1 or 2) do you think is nearer the truth? When you're suffering, how is the thought of reward after death a comfort to you?

4. Trials often serve as a breeding ground for temptations to sin. In such cases, we should not blame God for tempting us—indeed, He is the author only of good things—but instead we should blame ourselves if we give in to temptation.
   - Brandon thought he was marrying a Christian woman when he took Lynda to be his wife. But as it turned out, she wanted nothing to do with God and ridiculed Brandon for going to church and praying. After two and a half years of

a struggle to keep their marriage together, Lynda moved in with one of Brandon's friends. A divorce is now pending. What temptations is Brandon likely to face in the midst of this trial?

- Why is the reaction of many of us, when tempted, to blame God instead of to assume responsibility for our own actions? What sort of "death" will sin give birth to, if we have first allowed our lust to give birth to sin?

- Time yourself: In sixty seconds, name out loud as many of the good things God has given you as you can think of.

5. A true Christian is someone who demonstrates faith by solid, practical actions, living a holy life and helping others.

- Have you ever known anyone (perhaps yourself) who got too comfortable with being a Christian—went to church, hung out with other believers, but stopped doing anything as a result of his or her faith? What can give such a believer the bump he or she needs to start acting like a Christian?

- Together, brainstorm at least twenty *internal* acts of "doing the Word" (such as biting your tongue when you want to criticize someone) and at least twenty *external* acts of "doing the Word" (such as baby-sitting your neighbor's kids when she's sick).

Close in prayer asking God for wisdom in trials and in becoming more active Christians. Invite God's leading of the group throughout the rest of the journey you're sharing together.

Introduction to Unit 2
Wisdom in Friendships and Faith (James 2)

Destination: To understand that, regardless of what we say about the quality of our faith, our actions stand in judgment on our words.

Who among us does not still nurse debilitating wounds (at least a painful memory or two) from the classic grammar school ritual of choosing teams for kickball at recess? First, the teacher anointed her two favorites to be captains of the opposing teams. Next, she commissioned them to divide up the nonfavorites who stood quivering before them in fear and rejection. Not only had it just been proven that they were not among the two most worthy in the class, now they were about to find out just how unworthy they really were. Slowly, painfully, the anointed picked their favorites in what amounted to reverse-rejection order. And woe to that most nonfavorite, most rejected of all, the last person picked. Chosen just because he had a pulse, he knew that if the teacher hadn't been standing there, he wouldn't have been chosen at all.

Well, we all survived that recess ritual and went on to bigger and better things—especially the guy or girl who was chosen last (the one who shows up at the twenty-year high school reunion and announces he's buying "that crummy grade school and turning it into a shopping center"). But, laugh as we may about childhood bouts with favoritism, we know that it exists far beyond grammar school. In fact, adults—even Christian adults—are tempted to play favorites even when they know better.

James apparently knew better, and very possibly from firsthand experience. He wrote in the second chapter of his letter that playing favorites had no place in the community of the faithful. In fact, favoritism comes close to negating faith. In Acts 6 we discover that the church in Jerusalem, over which James eventually assumed leadership, was guilty of playing favorites. As the church grew in its early days, the believers, almost entirely Jewish, pooled their resources to meet one another's needs (Acts 2:44-45). Soon the church looked like a grade-school playground: the Hebraic Jews against the Hellenistic Jews. It seems that the widows among the Hellenistic Jews were being overlooked by those distributing the food (probably overseen by Jerusalem-based, Hebraic Jews). The result was the first committee in the history of the church: seven men, "full of the Spirit and of wisdom," to make sure the food was distributed evenly among all the needy, including the Hellenistic widows (Acts 6:1-3).

This appears to have made an impact on James. He is not mentioned in connection with this incident, but we know that he became the leader of the Jerusalem church in due course. It is therefore probably not accidental that James mentioned widows and favoritism in the same breath in his letter, though they are divided artificially by our modern chapter divisions (James

1:27–2:1). The uniting of those two themes is perhaps a clue to James' memory of the early days in the church—a memory he did not want to see reinforced by a continuation of the same practice in the dispersed church.

And why not, specifically? Because favoritism is sin, and sin diminishes the testimony of faith (James 2:9). Simply put, when we willingly sin in a single thing like favoritism, we may as well quit talking about our faith, because "faith without works is dead" (James 2:26).

Were you the last chosen on the playground? Not to worry. God doesn't play favorites. But, James said, if you want to be His friend, you need to put your feet where your faith is (match your walk with your talk), and not play favorites either (James 2:23). Good advice for recess—and for religion.

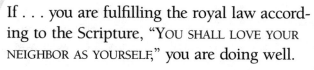 If . . . you are fulfilling the royal law according to the Scripture, "YOU SHALL LOVE YOUR NEIGHBOR AS YOURSELF," you are doing well.

JAMES 2:8

DAY 1

HOW TO BE A GOOD FRIEND TO EVERYONE

DON'T PLAY FAVORITES

Ever the plainspoken prophet, James put the truth on the bottom shelf where all can reach it freely: Don't play favorites.[52]

What is favoritism? It's easy to confuse favoritism with preferences, opinions, and desires, none of which are wrong or sinful. For instance, when you are planning a social activity and think of the names of several close friends whom you'd like to invite, that's not favoritism. It's just the normal human activity of building relationships and spending relaxed time with those with whom you share common interests. On the other hand, what if you are invited by a fellow believer to participate in an activity and you decline for the following reasons: You and the other person don't travel in the same social circles; you worry about what your friends might think of you when they discover you attended; by attending, you don't want to suggest to the person that you are interested in developing a relationship. Now we're in the realm of favoritism.

The Greek word for favoritism is actually a combination of two words: "to accept" and "face."[T20] In other words, favoritism is accepting or rejecting on the basis of the "face," or the appearance. To expand, it's accepting or rejecting a person on the basis of outward considerations of social status, economic standing, education, race or ethnicity, or any other prejudicial preference.

James didn't just forbid favoritism. With what did he suggest it is inconsistent?[52]

Why is favoritism inconsistent with professing faith in Christ?

WHO MADE YOU THE JUDGE?

James presented a hypothetical situation that was familiar to his original readers. It was probably common in Jewish synagogues[T21] for the wealthy, more prominent members to be escorted to the best seats,[53] while poorer attendees were asked to stand or sit on the floor.[54] We don't know this for

---

[52] **JAMES 2**
1 My brethren, do not hold your faith in our glorious Lord Jesus Christ with an attitude of personal favoritism.

[53] **MATTHEW 23**
6 "They love the place of honor at banquets and the chief seats in the synagogues."

[54] **JAMES 2**
2-3 If a man comes into your assembly with a gold ring and dressed in fine clothes, and there also comes in a poor man in dirty clothes, and you pay special attention to the one who is wearing the fine clothes, and say, "You sit here in a good place," and you say to the poor man, "You stand over there, or sit down by my footstool," . . .

[55] **JAMES 2**
4 Have you not made distinctions among yourselves, and become judges with evil motives?

[56] **MATTHEW 7**
1-2 "Do not judge so that you will not be judged. For in the way you judge, you will be judged; and by your standard of measure, it will be measured to you."

[57] **MATTHEW 7; ROMANS 2**
Matthew 7:5 "You hypocrite, first take the log out of your own eye, and then you will see clearly to take the speck out of your brother's eye."
Romans 2:1 You have no excuse, everyone of you who passes judgment, for in that which you judge another, you condemn yourself; for you who judge practice the same things.

sure, but perhaps some of James' readers had suffered under the hand of favoritism in Jerusalem. Now they found themselves as a curious minority in foreign lands. Their assemblies, or churches, would likely be visited by leaders in the community to investigate this new messianic form of Judaism. If they courted the wealthy and prominent members by showing them favoritism, they would be no better than the ones who had made them sit on the floor in their own synagogues back home. Or perhaps some of James' readers were wealthy themselves and were showing favoritism to wealthy visitors to their assemblies.

How did James describe those who show favoritism?[55]

What did his half brother, Jesus, have to say about judging?[56]

What is the key issue that makes judging another (favoritism) sinful?[57]

As we read in Matthew 23 (see appendix A), Jesus gave a lengthy discourse to the Pharisees on their hypocritical lifestyle. Read that chapter and answer the following questions:

• What were the Pharisees focused on (verses 5-7)?

• What word did Jesus use consistently to describe them (verses 13-15,23,25,27,29)?

In Jesus' words about final judgment, who ends up in a bad situation?[58]

It seems clear that hypocritical judging and showing favoritism are sinful. But aren't there times when Scripture encourages us to judge, to separate crowds into groups?

LANGUAGE & LIT:[T20]

FACE UP TO FAVORITISM—The Greek word for favoritism is *prosopolempsia* (if it was as hard to do as it is to pronounce, we wouldn't see it very often!). It comes from the words for "face" (*prosopon*) and "receive, accept" (*lambano*). Next time you find yourself tempted to show favoritism toward a person, imagine him or her without a "face" (or whatever characteristics you are using as criteria). If this person was a "generic" Christian believer, would you be favoring him or her?

HISTORY & CULTURE:[T21]

SYNAGOGUES—Synagogues probably arose during the period of the Babylonian exile (sixth century BC) as places for the assembly of Jews for instruction in the Scriptures. Since worship and sacrifice could only be conducted at the temple in Jerusalem, the synagogues were primarily places of instruction. Even after the return of the exiles, the synagogues remained in place and we see them mentioned frequently in the four Gospels and Acts. James' use of the word *sunagoge* ("synagogue," James 2:2) is significant since it is not used in any other New Testament letter. His use of "synagogue" to describe a place where Christians meet indicates the early date of his writing and his Jewish heritage.

[58]**MATTHEW 24**

51 "[The master] will cut [the slave] in pieces and assign him a place with the hypocrites; in that place there will be weeping and gnashing of teeth."

[59]**JAMES 2**

5-7 Listen, my beloved brethren: did not God choose the poor of this world to be rich in faith and heirs of the kingdom which He promised to those who love Him? But you have dishonored the poor man. Is it not the rich who oppress you and personally drag you into court? Do they not blaspheme the fair name by which you have been called?

Read the following verses and note the situations in which we are to be judges:

- 1 Corinthians 5:9,11: "I wrote you in my letter not to associate with immoral people. . . . Actually, I wrote to you not to associate with any so-called brother if he is an immoral person, or covetous, or an idolater, or a reviler, or a drunkard, or a swindler—not even to eat with such a one."

- 1 Corinthians 11:28: "A man must examine himself, and in so doing he is to eat of the bread and drink of the cup."

- 2 Corinthians 11:12-15: "What I am doing I will continue to do, so that I may cut off opportunity from those who desire an opportunity to be regarded just as we are in the matter about which they are boasting. For such men are false apostles, deceitful workers, disguising themselves as apostles of Christ. No wonder, for even Satan disguises himself as an angel of light. Therefore it is not surprising if his servants also disguise themselves as servants of righteousness, whose end will be according to their deeds."

- Philippians 3:2: "Beware of the dogs, beware of the evil workers, beware of the false circumcision."

- 1 Thessalonians 5:21: "Examine everything carefully; hold fast to that which is good."

- 1 John 4:1-6: "Beloved, do not believe every spirit, but test the spirits to see whether they are from God, because many false prophets have gone out into the world. By this you know the Spirit of God: every spirit that confesses that Jesus Christ has come in the flesh is from God; and every spirit that does not confess Jesus is not from God; this is the spirit of the antichrist, of which you have heard that it is coming, and now it is already in the world. You are from God, little children, and have overcome them; because greater is He who is in you than he who is in the world. They are from the world; therefore they speak as from the world, and the world listens to them. We are from God; he who knows God listens to us; he who is not from God does not listen to us. By this we know the spirit of truth and the spirit of error."

- 2 John 10: "If anyone comes to you and does not bring this teaching, do not receive him into your house, and do not give him a greeting."

Describe a time in your own Christian experience when you discovered yourself showing, or tempted to show, favoritism.

Has there been a time when you were forced to make a judgment (in the way encouraged by Scripture) on a moral or theological basis? What happened?

GOD'S "FAVORITES"

More than one pileup has occurred at the intersection of money (or the lack of it) and the spiritual life. Some, following the model of Jesus, think modesty, even poverty, is the kingdom way. Others would say that the amount of money one has is irrelevant (meaning wealth is acceptable), that the issue is one's attitude toward it. James jumped into this fray, but for a different purpose. His concern was not to settle the question of whether having money is more acceptable to God than not having it.[T22] He was very concerned, however, about how Christians respond to people who have money. Let's figure out what he was saying in verses 5-7:[59]

Who was he talking to (verse 5)?

What had they done (verse 6)?[T23]

What kind of people had they been showing favoritism to (verse 7)?

BRINGING IT HOME

1. Describe in your own words what James was concerned about in 2:1-7.

2. Why do you think people favor the rich when it is the poor who need "favors"?

3. How do you think God wants you to relate to the poor and the rich whom He has placed around you? How do you evaluate their varying needs?

CROSS REFERENCES:[T22]

THE POWER OF MONEY—The possession of money per se is neither condemned nor affirmed in Scripture. What is addressed is the power that money provides to those who possess it. The use of power, therefore, is the issue. Having much money affords one great power; having no money leaves one powerless. Those with money are tempted to oppress the powerless; those without money are often defenseless against the rich. It is the oppression of the poor, rather than the support of the poor, with which God takes issue.

For further study:
Leviticus 25:35-43; Matthew 6:19-24; Mark 12:42-44; Luke 19:8-9; 2 Corinthians 8–9; Philippians 4:11,19; 1 Timothy 6:3-10

POINT OF INTEREST:[T23]

DISHONORING THE POOR—James took his Jewish brothers and sisters to task for something he knew was close to God's heart: They had dishonored (insulted) the poor. The Mosaic Law had specific provisions for the care of the poor: Exodus 22:22-27; 23:11; Leviticus 19:9-10,13,15; 25:25-30; Ruth 2:1-7. Israel itself had been redeemed out of great poverty in Egypt—a fact kept before them at all times (1 Kings 8:50-53). Israel's failure to keep the covenant resulted in poverty in the nation (Deuteronomy 15:4-11). The wrongs done to the poor concerned the prophets, and they railed against such abuses constantly (Isaiah 1:23; 10:1-2; Ezekiel 34; Amos 2:6; 5:7; 8:6; Micah 2:1-2; Habakkuk 3:14; Malachi 3:5). For Christians to dishonor the poor is to come close to insulting the priorities of God.

DAILY READING

Read Matthew 6:1-18 (see appendix A) and mark those verses that support what you have read in James today.

[60]**JAMES 2**
9 If you show partiality, you are committing sin and are convicted by the law as transgressors.

[61]**JAMES 2**
8 If . . . you are fulfilling the royal law according to the Scripture, "YOU SHALL LOVE YOUR NEIGHBOR AS YOURSELF," you are doing well.

[62]**MATTHEW 22**
37-40 [Jesus] said to [the lawyer], " 'YOU SHALL LOVE THE LORD YOUR GOD WITH ALL YOUR HEART, AND WITH ALL YOUR SOUL, AND WITH ALL YOUR MIND.' This is the great and foremost commandment. The second is like it, 'YOU SHALL LOVE YOUR NEIGHBOR AS YOURSELF.' On these two commandments depend the whole Law and the Prophets."

[63]**EXODUS 20**
3-4,7-8,12-17 You shall have no other gods before Me. You shall not make for yourself an idol. . . . You shall not take the name of the Lord your God in vain. . . . Remember the sabbath day, to keep it holy. . . . Honor your father and your mother. . . . You shall not murder. You shall not commit adultery. You shall not steal. You shall not bear false witness against your neighbor. You shall not covet.

DAY 2

WHY TO AVOID PLAYING FAVORITES

Deciding what course of action to take in the Christian life can sometimes be difficult. There are many decisions we face that simply are not covered in Scripture: who to marry, where to live, how much money to give to charity and the Lord's work, how many children to have, where to go to college, and on and on. Those decisions require prayer, counsel, the study of scriptural principles, and then stepping out in faith.

But many other issues in the spiritual life are plain: God has revealed His will on these matters in no uncertain terms. And to violate His will when it is given plainly to us is to find ourselves in sin, and thereby guilty of breaking His Laws. Such was the case in the matter that James was addressing to his readers: showing favoritism.[60] In the next section of his letter, however, he addressed favoritism from a different perspective—that of the person who *isn't* shown favor, the excluded or unloved one. Not to love one's neighbor (or friend or family member) is to violate God's clear directives.

HOW TO DO WELL

Many things in life are binary, meaning they have only two positions. The switches in transistors on computer chips are either open or closed. Light switches are either on or off. Law is like that—you keep it or you don't. Granted, there are mitigating circumstances in trying to keep any law, but there are really only two positions: Did you keep the Law or violate it? In this section of his letter, James covered both positions with regard to the requirement to keep the "royal law" of Scripture,[T24] loving one's neighbor as oneself.[61]

What is the "royal law" of Scripture?

Why do you think James called it the "royal" law?[T25]

When Jesus was asked by someone what the greatest commandment in the Law is, He said there are two commandments under which all the rest of God's standards can be summarized.[62]

What is the "great and foremost commandment"?

What is the second "great" commandment?

The reason Jesus said that all the Law could be summarized under these two commands is that they summarize the Ten Commandments God gave through Moses.[T26] The first four of the Ten Commandments have to do with loving God, the last six with loving your neighbor.[63] Summarize each of the Ten Commandments under its proper heading.

Love God	Love Your Neighbor
1.	5.
2.	6.
3.	7.
4.	8.
	9.
	10.

Write the shortest sentence you can summarizing humankind's two central obligations in life.

The apostle Paul beautifully expounded on Jesus' words in his letter to the believers in Rome (see Romans 13:8-10).[64] In his words, if you have loved your neighbor, what have you done with regard to the Law?

How would you evaluate favoritism in light of the "royal law" to love one's neighbor?

How Not to Do Well

We said the Law was binary—you either keep it or you don't. You do well if you keep the Law; you don't do well if you don't keep it. Two things remain for us to understand James' discussion of favoritism in light of God's expectations (His Law) for humankind.

CROSS REFERENCES:[T24]
LOVE AND HATE—James quoted from Leviticus 19:18: "You shall not take vengeance, nor bear any grudge against the sons of your people, but you shall love your neighbor as yourself; I am the LORD." By Jesus' day, some strict Pharisees had added a corollary, "Hate your enemies," feeling it was implied by Leviticus 19:18. Jesus corrected that in Matthew 5:43-44 ("You have heard that it was said, 'YOU SHALL LOVE YOUR NEIGHBOR and hate your enemy. But I say to you, love your enemies."), shocking the Jewish world with the extent of His emphasis on love.

LANGUAGE & LIT:[T25]
THE KING OF LAWS—In the phrase "royal law" (James 2:8), "royal" is a translation of *basilikos*. (Do you recognize our English *basilica*, referring to a Catholic church that has been accorded privileged status by the pope?) The Greek word means "kingly." A king is over all others, and the law of love is over all other laws governing relationships. Therefore, the law of love is the "royal law."

POINT OF INTEREST:[T26]
MOST, FEWER, FEWEST—It is interesting to note the pyramid of law as given by God to the nation of Israel. At the bottom of the pyramid there are more than 630 individual statutes and commandments governing Israel's civil, moral, and religious life. Near the top of the pyramid, the number given to Moses narrows to ten, the Ten Commandments, which serve as a summary of the moral law. Finally, Jesus summarized the ten into two: Love God and love your neighbor.

[64]**ROMANS 13**

8-10 Owe nothing to anyone except to love one another; for he who loves his neighbor has fulfilled the law. For this, "YOU SHALL NOT COMMIT ADULTERY, YOU SHALL NOT MURDER, YOU SHALL NOT STEAL, YOU SHALL NOT COVET," and if there is any other commandment, it is summed up in this saying, "YOU SHALL LOVE YOUR NEIGHBOR AS YOURSELF." Love does no wrong to a neighbor; therefore love is the fulfillment of the law.

[65]**LUKE 10**

29 Wishing to justify himself, [a lawyer] said to Jesus, "And who is my neighbor?"

[66]**JAMES 2**

10-11 Whoever keeps the whole law and yet stumbles in one point, he has become guilty of all. For He who said, "DO NOT COMMIT ADULTERY," also said, "DO NOT COMMIT MURDER." Now if you do not commit adultery, but do commit murder, you have become a transgressor of the law.

First, who is my neighbor? That is, am I expected to love everyone the same—no exceptions? (In the context of James, is favoritism always sin?) This is the question a lawyer asked Jesus after hearing about the second great commandment.[65] Jesus' reply was in the form of the well-known story of the good Samaritan.[T27]

Read that story in Luke 10:30-37 (see appendix A). In essence, what was Jesus' answer to the question "Who is my neighbor?"

Using this definition—"My neighbor is anyone with a need that I can meet"—what was James saying to his readers about seating arrangements in church on Sunday morning? If love (the "royal law") is extended to each person who enters, rich or poor, how will seating arrangements be handled?

Second, James addressed the hypocritical notion that it might be acceptable to show favoritism (or commit any other "minor" sin) as long as I am not breaking any of the "big" commandments. What was his conclusion regarding this idea?[66]

Because God is one (Deuteronomy 6:4), His will is one as well. To violate only one part of His will is to "become a transgressor of the law."[66] An analogy is the church, the body of believers in Christ. If you weep, we all weep. If you rejoice, we all rejoice (Romans 12:15). The whole is affected by each of its parts (1 Corinthians 12:26).

BRINGING IT HOME

1. Make a list of all your neighbors (those people with a need you can meet).

2. According to the "royal law of Scripture," what should you try to do for these neighbors?

3. Have you been tempted, as apparently James' audience was, to consider that keeping some of God's "bigger" laws as a Christian exempted you from keeping a smaller law like showing love to a neighbor? What are those "bigger laws" that Christians keep in order to defend themselves against the accusations of their conscience for not loving a neighbor?

4. Since James says we are lawbreakers when we don't keep the "royal law," is there any failure to keep God's law of love that you need to confess to Him? Write out a brief prayer here, receive His forgiveness, and then seek out a neighbor to love.

HISTORY & CULTURE:[T27]
SAMARITANS—A historic and ongoing animosity existed between Jews and Samaritans. When the Jews of the ten northern tribes of Israel were carried into captivity by Assyria in the eighth century BC, the Jews left behind were intermarried with conquering Assyrians who took up residence in the northern region of Israel. This "half-breed" status was a great offense to Jews in Judea. By the time of Christ, a faithful Jew would not even venture into Samaria (between Judea and Galilee), much less talk to a Samaritan. Thus, Jesus' encounter with a Samaritan woman (John 4) and His story of the good Samaritan (Luke 10) are all the more extraordinary (especially since He had been accused of being a demon-possessed Samaritan Himself, John 8:48).

DAILY READING

Read Matthew 5:43-48 (see appendix A). Mark those verses that correlate best with what James teaches in this part of his letter.

[67]**JAMES 2**

13 For judgment will be merciless to one who has shown no mercy; mercy triumphs over judgment.

[68]**JAMES 2**

12 So speak and so act as those who are to be judged by the law of liberty.

[69]**JOHN 5**

24 "Truly, truly, I say to you, he who hears My word, and believes Him who sent Me, has eternal life, and does not come into judgment, but has passed out of death into life."

[70]**1 CORINTHIANS 3**

12-15 If any man builds on the foundation with gold, silver, precious stones, wood, hay, straw, each man's work will become evident; for the day will show it because it is to be revealed with fire, and the fire itself will test the quality of each man's work. If any man's work which he has built on it remains, he will receive a reward. If any man's work is burned up, he will suffer loss; but he himself will be saved, yet so as through fire.

[71]**2 CORINTHIANS 5**

10 We must all appear before the judgment seat of Christ, so that each one may be recompensed for his deeds in the body, according to what he has done, whether good or bad.

[72]**REVELATION 22**

12 "Behold, I am coming quickly, and My reward is with Me, to render to every man according to what he has done."

DAY 3

PREPARE TO BE JUDGED MERCIFULLY

When was the last time you heard anything from a pulpit about the judgment to come? Perhaps in our desire to be relevant, upbeat, and nonoffensive to the world, the concept of a future judgment has been toned down in Christian preaching. Perhaps we're on the far side of a pendulum swing that began in the days of the Puritans, the days that heard Jonathan Edwards preach "Sinners in the Hands of an Angry God" in eighteenth-century New England.[T28] But that and other Puritan sermons helped ignite the Great Awakening, which swept the eastern seaboard of America from 1725 to 1760. Perhaps preaching about the judgment to come isn't such a bad idea.

James, for one, would agree. After giving clear instruction to the dispersed church about the sin of favoritism (the failure to be loving and merciful), he added a pregnant "For . . ."[67] There's always a "because" that drives the message home. We learn from our mothers not to touch the stove, because . . . And James was about to tell us why we shouldn't be judgmental and unmerciful in our dealings with others.

HOW TO ACT

"So speak and so act,"[68] James said emphatically. In the particular situation he started out addressing (James 2:2-4), he meant, "Don't turn away from the less prominent and less fortunate members who enter the church. Speak enthusiastically and generously to them, and escort them to the best seats you have available. And do the same when the prominent and fortunate members enter as well. Treat them all the same—with love."

When we see a person acting like that, we know he or she is a person who is free to love everyone, a person who lives by a law that gives liberty and freedom—"the law of liberty"[68]—as opposed to a legalistic or moralistic code that enslaves, such as that which the scribes and Pharisees in James' day had created.[T29]

What would motivate a person to love that way? James' words in verse 12 give the answer:[68] We are going to be judged by the law of liberty. In other words, we are going to be judged by a law of love and mercy that will judge us according to the love and mercy we have shown others.

Is that true? What do you think the prevailing notion is among Christians concerning future judgment? Are they expecting any?

What does John 5:24 offer by way of assurance concerning a Christian's salvation?[69]

What do each of the following verses say about a Christian's future judgment?

- 1 Corinthians 3:12-15[70]

- 2 Corinthians 5:10[71, T30]

- Revelation 22:12[72]

James was not talking about judgment to determine our eternal destiny, heaven or hell. Rather, he was talking about the rewards that come to believers (or not) on the basis of what we have done in this life with the gift of our salvation.

What do Jesus' words add to your understanding of how God will look upon us at the end of our life?

- Matthew 5:7;[73] 7:1-2[56]

HISTORY & CULTURE:[T28]

GREAT AWAKENINGS—The Puritan preacher Jonathan Edwards (said by many to be the most brilliant American theologian in history) turned New England upside down on July 8, 1741. In Enfield, Connecticut, he preached his sermon "Sinners in the Hands of an Angry God"—7,176 words on Deuteronomy 32:35, "Their foot shall slide in due time." Among other things, he told his audience,

Your wickedness makes you as it were heavy as lead, and to tend downwards with great weight and pressure towards hell; and if God should let you go, you would immediately sink and swiftly descend and plunge into the bottomless gulf, and your healthy constitution, and your own care and prudence, and best contrivance, and all your righteousness, would have no more influence to uphold you and keep you out of hell, than a spider's web would have to stop a falling rock. . . . The God that holds you over the pit of hell, much as one holds a spider, or some loathsome insect over the fire, abhors you, and is dreadfully provoked: his wrath towards you burns like fire; he looks upon you as worthy of nothing else, but to be cast into the fire; he is of purer eyes than to bear to have you in his sight; you are ten thousand times more abominable in his eyes, than the most hateful venomous serpent is in ours.

In case you're wondering if sermons on judgment can motivate people to action, it is said that by the end of this sermon (which he read in a monotone voice) there were few in the pews not crying out for mercy from God.

[73]MATTHEW 5
7 "Blessed are the merciful, for they shall receive mercy."

[74]MATTHEW 6
14-15 "If you forgive others for their transgressions, your heavenly Father will also forgive you. But if you do not forgive others, then your Father will not forgive your transgressions."

[75]MATTHEW 18
33,35 "'Should you not also have had mercy on your fellow slave, in the same way that I had mercy on you?' . . . My heavenly Father will also do the same to you, if each of you does not forgive his brother from your heart."

[76]EPHESIANS 4
32 Be kind to one another, tender-hearted, forgiving each other, just as God in Christ also has forgiven you.

[77]GALATIANS 5
22 The fruit of the Spirit is love . . .

• Matthew 6:14-15[74]

• Matthew 18:33,35[75]

WHY TO ACT

Now back to James' words in verse 12.[68] If you know *ahead of time* (which you now do) that God is going to be as merciful toward you as you have been toward others, how does that affect your motivation to live lovingly toward all, not showing favoritism toward any?

It should have a powerful effect on our behavior, "for . . ." (fill in what James gives as the reason from verse 13):[67]

How does it make you feel to know that one day God might evaluate your life without mercy because you did not show mercy to others?

What did James say has power over judgment in the final analysis?[67] What does it mean that "mercy triumphs over judgment"?

BRINGING IT HOME

1. What insight does Romans 3:10-18 (see appendix A) offer concerning your ability to love as James was talking about—and thereby receive merciful judgment?

2. What example of mercy and love have you been shown that sets a standard for your love for others?[76] What source of power has God provided to help you love consistently?[77]

3. Would it make any difference in the quality of love manifested by Christians if the truth of future judgment were taught more frequently? Be honest—were you aware that you were going to be evaluated by God one day, and that your own love for others would be the measuring stick He would use? How has this truth changed your thinking? How will it change your actions?

CROSS REFERENCES:[T29]

BURDENSOME LAWS—The law of liberty to which James referred was the hallmark of Jesus' ministry—the emphasis on love (John 13:35). Jesus confronted the Pharisees often about the hundreds of manmade traditions and laws they had created for the purpose of earning righteousness before God (Matthew 23:23; Mark 7:1-13) and setting themselves up as authorities before men. It was in response to this situation (which began in Israel hundreds of years earlier; see Ezekiel 34) that Jesus said, "Come to Me, all who are weary and heavy-laden, and I will give you rest. Take My yoke upon you and learn from Me, for I am gentle and humble in heart, and YOU WILL FIND REST FOR YOUR SOULS" (Matthew 11:28-29). What is the state of your own soul? Are you enveloped in love or in law? If the latter, go to Jesus.

LANGUAGE & LIT:[T30]

JUDGMENT SEAT OF CHRIST—The judgment seat of Christ (or "of God"; Romans 14:10) is the *bema*, a raised platform in Greek courts where the legal representatives of the accused and accuser took their stand. All believers will one day stand before the *bema* of Christ to be rewarded or diminished for the quality of faithfulness to Christ while on this earth.

DAILY READING

Read Matthew 18:21-35 (see appendix A). Mark the key verses that parallel James' words in this section of his letter.

[78] **JAMES 2**

14 What use is it, my brethren, if someone says he has faith but he has no works? Can that faith save him?

[79] **JAMES 2**

15-16 If a brother or sister is without clothing and in need of daily food, and one of you says to them, "Go in peace, be warmed and be filled," and yet you do not give them what is necessary for their body, what use is that?

[80] **JAMES 2**

17 Faith, if it has no works, is dead, being by itself.

DAY 4

DOES YOUR FAITH HAVE A PULSE?

What's the first thing an emergency room attendant looks for when a trauma victim is rushed to the hospital? A pulse. Regardless of how damaged a person's body is and how precariously he is clinging to life, if there is a pulse, there is hope. When there is no pulse, there is no life, and without life, there is no future. So the pulse is the key to it all. And James said, in this section of his letter, that there is a pulse—an indicator—in the spiritual life as well.

James was turning a corner in his letter. The first thirteen verses of chapter 2 (covered in the first three days of unit 2 in this GUIDEBOOK), dealt with the failure to love others unconditionally. Here he continued that general theme, but at a deeper level. Now he will say that the failure to love (or manifest other good works) may be a sign of a bigger problem. James gave his readers the benefit of the doubt in the first part of chapter 1—he assumed disobedience or ignorance was the problem where favoritism existed. Now he said something more serious. In an absence of good works, it may be time to check for a pulse. There may be no life there at all.

THE PURPOSE OF FAITH

When we discuss faith and good works at the same time, it's like putting two primary colors next to each other— they look differently together than when you see them separately. To see why, start by writing your own definition of faith (hint: James gives you a clue in 2:14).[78]

Remember our discussion of binary events in day 2 of this unit—events that are either black or white, on or off, right or wrong? Your definition of faith should have reflected that kind of definition, because the purpose of faith is to save you. You are either saved (you possess eternal life) or you're not (you don't possess eternal life)—there is nothing in between. Good works, on the other hand, are a million shades of gray: Anybody's efforts to love and serve others could be evaluated as good, better, or best depending on who's doing the evaluating.

Draw a line from salvation and good works to the term that best describes them:

Salvation is . . .   Subjective

Good works are . . .   Objective

All of this has been to demonstrate why this portion of James' letter must be navigated carefully. When establishing the presence of something objective using subjective evidence, there is room for error.[T31]

AN EXAMPLE

In this section of the letter, James was putting an objective thing (faith) next to a subjective thing (good works) to show how good works, in the final analysis, have to be taken as evidence for the existence of a living, dynamic faith. Before going further, what again is the purpose of faith?

The purpose of faith is to _____ you.[78]

And if good works are an evidence of faith, then good works are an evidence (in some way—and this is part of the problem) of whether you are truly _____ .

Therefore, if your eternal salvation is in some way reflected by your good works, how important would it be to you personally to understand this connection? Why?

Read James' example (it is based in church life just like his previous illustration about favoritism) and explain the conflict James was illustrating (note that his example doesn't mention faith; it's simply a basic contradiction between what is needed and what is accomplished in a certain situation).[79]

When James asked, "What use is that?" (verse 16), he was setting up his key conclusion, found in the next verse.[80] We'll begin verse 17 with the question he asked at the end of verse 16, and you fill in the rest from verse 17 in your own words:

What use is faith that _____?
We could say that that kind of faith is

_____.

POINT OF INTEREST:[T31]

INTERNAL VS. EXTERNAL— Misunderstanding the relationship between objective faith and subjective good works has caused (and still causes) enormous theological error. For instance, the Pharisees wanted to objectify good works as a way to evaluate who was spiritual and who was not. They created hundreds, if not thousands, of small religious rules in order to compartmentalize an endless variety of good works and thus be able to observe who had done them (and, by implication, who was spiritual). They even went to the extent of cutting their herbs (dill, mint, cummin) into equal parts in order to give a tenth of them to the temple service. This was objective—countable, measurable—which they liked. But when it came to subjective requirements of the Law, such as justice, mercy, and faithfulness, they ignored those, Jesus said (Matthew 23:23).

Theologically, what the gospel introduced that the Pharisees (both ancient and modern) missed was sanctification—the doctrine that we become and act better over time once we have crossed from nonfaith to faith. Our faith is demonstrated gradually as we walk with Christ. We rest not in a completed checklist of religious works but in the grace of God assuring us that we are His children and that He is patient with our efforts to please Him more and more each day. It is when the desire to please Him is absent that we should be concerned.

81 **JAMES 2**

18 Someone may well say, "You have faith and I have works; show me your faith without the works, and I will show you my faith by my works."

82 **JAMES 2**

19 You believe that God is one. You do well; the demons also believe, and shudder.

If we try to evaluate the "aliveness" of our faith (an objective thing) by the presence or absence of good works (a subjective thing), what problems will we encounter?

If a person's faith is only valid based on the quality of his or her good works, how could anyone ever be sure of salvation? What quality of works is sufficient to be saved?

You can see that faith and good works together become a complicated subject. But James would not allow them to be separated. In day 5, we will see how to keep them together without confusing their respective meanings in James' letter. To conclude, James issued a challenge to those who think they can have "either/or," when James wanted to have "both/and."

A CHALLENGE

Bible translators have handled verse 18 differently (the quote in it is either short or long, depending on the Bible version).[81, T32] In essence, James was suggesting that an objector speaks up and says, "Faith, works—some have one, some the other. It's not necessary to have both."

When he said, "Show me your faith without the works," what was he implying by his challenge?

How was he willing to prove his own faith?

With whom did James categorize people who boast in their belief in God but who have no works to validate their belief?[82]

BRINGING IT HOME

1. Based on what you have learned in this lesson, add what you would say next in the following conversation with a friend.

   You: "John, what sort of ministry are you involved in?"

   John: "None. I don't feel it's my calling to get involved in other people's lives. God is happy with me because I believe in Him."

   You:

2. Have you ever had the experience of someone asking you what is behind the quality of your life (the "good works" that your life manifests)? If so, how did good works serve as an evidence of your faith? If not, what does that make you contemplate regarding the "pulse" of your faith?[T33]

LANGUAGE & LIT:[T32]

JAMES 2:18—Comparing the *New American Standard Bible* (NASB; the version used in this GUIDEBOOK) with the *New International Version* (NIV) illustrates the two basic possibilities for this verse. The NIV limits the quote (what James' hypothetical objector says) to the first part of verse 18: "But someone will say, 'You have faith; I have deeds.'" The NASB includes a larger part of the verse in the quote (see Road Map note 81). Fortunately, the choice doesn't radically impinge on our ability to sense James' meaning. But it does illustrate the challenges faced by translators since original Greek manuscripts included no punctuation.

CROSS REFERENCES:[T33]

WHEN GOD IS WITH US—Zechariah 8:23 foretells a day in the future when men from all the nations (Gentiles) "will grasp the garment of a Jew, saying, 'Let us go with you, for we have heard that God is with you.'" When people see by our lives that "God is with us," they often attach themselves to us in order to find God! Nicodemus risked his reputation as a Jewish leader because of the works he saw Jesus doing (John 3:2). When was the last time someone risked his or her reputation among other unsaved people by seeking you out to discover the source of your good works?

DAILY READING

Read Matthew 25:34-40 (see appendix A). What do you see in this passage that parallels James' words about the importance of works as evidence of faith?

[83]JAMES 2

20 Are you willing to recognize, you foolish fellow, that faith without works is useless?

[84]GENESIS 15

6 [Abraham] believed in the LORD; and He reckoned it to him as righteousness.

[85]GENESIS 22

16-18 "By Myself I have sworn," declares the LORD, "because you have done this thing and have not withheld your son, your only son, indeed I will greatly bless you, and I will greatly multiply your seed as the stars of the heavens and as the sand which is on the seashore; and your seed shall possess the gate of their enemies. In your seed all the nations of the earth shall be blessed, because you have obeyed My voice."

[86]JAMES 2

21 Was not Abraham our father justified by works when he offered up Isaac his son on the altar?

[87]JAMES 2

22 You see that faith was working with his works, and as a result of the works, faith was perfected.

[88]ROMANS 5

1 Having been justified by faith, we have peace with God through our Lord Jesus Christ.

[89]GALATIANS 3

26 You are all sons of God through faith in Christ Jesus.

[90]EPHESIANS 2

8 By grace you have been saved through faith; and that not of yourselves, it is the gift of God.

DAY 5

HOW TO KNOW IF YOUR FAITH IS ALIVE

A trial in any courtroom in America will last only as long as the evidence is sound. Without evidence, you have no collar, no case, and no conviction. As we conclude the second chapter of James' letter, we see him marshalling a strong defense against his proposition that "faith, if it has no works, is dead" (James 2:17). His chief witness is none other than Abraham, the father of the Jewish nation.

EVIDENCE

James began with a strong rebuff to his hypothetical objector.[83, T34] If it is evidence that is needed (to prove that faith without works is dead), then evidence is what he would provide. James was referring to his previous statement in verse 17, but here, instead of "dead," he says faith without works is "useless." Say a suspension bridge across a wide river is started from one shore but is never met in the middle by an equal section from the other side. We could say that the bridge is "useless," couldn't we? Remember this illustration—James is about to make a similar point, that faith and works are useless without each other.

EXPLANATION

With the possible exception of Moses, no one is so revered in Judaism as Abraham. To offer his life as evidence of true faith would be to make a compelling case in the eyes of James' Jewish readers. There are two parts to Abraham's story that you must understand to get James' point. Read the following passages (see appendix A) and write down what happened to Abraham in each event:

- Genesis 15:1-6 (verse 6 is the key verse)[84]

- Genesis 22:1-18 (verses 16-18 are the key verses)[85]

The events leading up to Genesis 15 happened approximately thirty years before the events of Genesis 22. So what did Abraham do first, believe God (exercise faith) or obey God (do a good work)?

If you read only verse 21[86] by itself, does it seem that Abraham was saved by his faith or his works?

How does verse 22[87] explain (amplify) verse 21?

Recalling the bridge illustration (see page 56), think of faith and works as the two halves of a bridge that meet and allow commerce to take place over time. In that same sense, how do faith and works unite over time in the believer's life to allow spiritual "commerce" to flow?

WARNING! This illustration is good only up to a certain point, demonstrating that, over time, a person's Christian faith is completed and validated by his or her works. Pushed to the extreme, it implies that a person can't be saved without good works. But what is it that actually saves a person?

• Romans 5:1[88]

• Galatians 3:26[89]

• Ephesians 2:8[90]

So, was James in conflict with Paul? Are works necessary to be saved? No—Paul and James were of one accord in this matter for the following reasons:

People are justified (declared righteous) before God by faith.

People are justified (proved righteous) before other people by works.

If people are ever going to be found righteous before God, it will be only on the basis of faith. But if people are ever going to be proved faithful before other people, it will

LANGUAGE & LIT:[T34]

DIATRIBE—Occasionally, New Testament writers employed a literary technique known as diatribe. That technique was different from the diatribe we think of today—a lengthy, often angry, opinion or denunciation. Instead, it came in the form of questions and answers, arranged so as to wear away (the original meaning of "diatribe" in the Greek language) objections to a point being made. The writer would create a hypothetical objector and put questions in his mouth, which were then answered. Paul used this literary device in Romans on several occasions (Romans 3:1,3,5,9,27-31; 9:14, 19-20; 11:1,11).

POINT OF INTEREST:[T35]

EVIDENCE OF FAITH—The question is often asked by preachers, "If you were brought into court on charges of being a Christian, would there be enough evidence to convict you?" It's a good question but one that must be asked and answered carefully. The truth is that no one can judge the reality of the faith of another. We can only go by a person's confession (Romans 10:9) and behavior (James 2:22). God alone is the final judge (Romans 2:16; James 4:12). A proper use of passages such as these in James is to judge ourselves, not others. We should let them serve as a warning to us to examine our own faith more than the faith of others (1 Corinthians 9:27; 11:28; Hebrews 10:19-27).

[91] JAMES 2
24 You see that a man is justified by works and not by faith alone.

[92] EPHESIANS 2
10 We are His workmanship, created in Christ Jesus for good works, which God prepared beforehand so that we would walk in them.

[93] JAMES 2
23 The Scripture was fulfilled which says, "AND ABRAHAM BELIEVED GOD, AND IT WAS RECKONED TO HIM AS RIGHTEOUSNESS," and he was called the friend of God.

[94] ROMANS 5
10 If while we were enemies we were reconciled to God through the death of His Son, much more, having been reconciled, we shall be saved by His life.

[95] GALATIANS 5
19-21 The deeds of the flesh are evident, which are: immorality, impurity, sensuality, idolatry, sorcery, enmities, strife, jealousy, outbursts of anger, disputes, dissensions, factions, envying, drunkenness, carousing, and things like these, of which I forewarn you, just as I have forewarned you, that those who practice such things will not inherit the kingdom of God.

[96] JAMES 2
25 Was not Rahab the harlot . . . justified by works when she received the messengers and sent them out by another way?

[97] JAMES 2
26 Just as the body without the spirit is dead, so also faith without works is dead.

be on the basis of works. James was saying[91] (and Paul would agree[92]) that a faith without good works was never alive to begin with.

Evidence is the key to conviction when faith is on trial. The evidence of a genuine saving faith is deeds of righteousness. Over time, where there are no deeds, there is a reasonable doubt as to the presence of saving faith.[T35]

When belief was coupled with works (obedience to God) in Abraham's life, what kind of relationship did he then have with God?[93, T36]

To go to the opposite extreme, what could you call a person who did not obey God?[94]

What kind of works characterizes those people's lives?[95]

EXAMPLE

James concluded his connection between faith and works by citing someone whose faith is hardly mentioned in Scripture but whose works were huge—and who was justified as a result.[96] A prostitute who aided the nation of Israel because of her faith in God (Joshua 2:11) was considered a righteous person when she proved her faith with her works.[T37]

Based on James' final words in this section,[97] fill in the following analogy between the human body and faith:

The human body is animated (proved to be alive) by the human _____.

Faith is animated (proved to be alive) by _____.

BRINGING IT HOME

1. It's difficult to compare Rahab in a primitive period of Old Testament history with a contemporary Christian believer who has had the advantage of reading the New Testament's presentation of salvation by faith. But James was a New Testament author who seems to have commended Rahab's model of placing great emphasis on demonstrating faith by works. In the contemporary church, which seems to get the most emphasis—faith (how to become a Christian, and so on) or works (how to demonstrate your Christianity)?

2. What do you say when asked to share your "testimony"? Is it only about when you were saved? If your testimony is not more about the exciting things Christ is doing through you today (Mark 16:20) than about how you first believed in Him, it may be that the two halves of your bridge have not met. How would you assess the "works" part of your Christian life after reading this portion of James?

CROSS REFERENCES:[T36]

FRIENDSHIP WITH GOD—
Three times in Scripture Abraham is referred to as the friend of God, a title accorded no one else (2 Chronicles 20:7; Isaiah 41:8; James 2:23). "Friend" was a covenant term implying the deepest loyalty (see 2 Samuel 16:17; Psalm 41:9; Proverbs 17:17; 27:6; 27:10). Friends were even closer than brothers (Proverbs 18:24) because they were bound by covenant oaths (1 Samuel 20:42). Jonathan broke allegiance with his father, Saul, in order to remain faithful to his covenant friend, David (1 Samuel 20). Even Jesus said that His true family was made up of those who did the will of God (Matthew 12:46-50)—those whom He also described as His friends (John 15:14-15). True friendship is demonstrated by a willingness to meet the needs of a friend, whatever the needs might be (1 Samuel 20:4; John 15:7).

HISTORY & CULTURE:[T37]

RAHAB—History has remembered Rahab in the same way as greats of the faith such as Noah, Abraham, Sarah, Isaac, Jacob, Joseph, Moses, Gideon, and others. In Hebrews 11, the "Hall of Faith" chapter in the Bible, Rahab is remembered for the faith she displayed in aiding the people of God (Hebrews 11:31). This doesn't signal approval of her profession but rather stands as a testimony that God's grace is able to transform the works of the flesh into the works of the kingdom in anyone's life.

DAILY READING

Read Hebrews 11 (see appendix A) and mark every instance where works are cited as an evidence of faith.

To the leader: Gather supplies for the creative Bible story presentations in step 5.

1. Evidently James had gotten wind that some of his first readers were kowtowing to rich folks—and this in spite of the fact that it was the rich who had been causing them problems! James condemned showing favoritism on the basis of social standing.
   • How many siblings were there in your birth family, and where did you come in the order? Did you think your parents' had a favorite among the children? How does it feel to be overlooked?
   • If a well-dressed person showed up for a meeting among James' first readers, they would show him to one of the best seats. In today's church, what are some similar ways of showing favoritism to the well-off? What might be the effects of such behavior on poorer church members?
   • Do you think James was saying we should show a preference for the poor, or that we should treat everyone exactly the same? Explain your interpretation.

2. Would James' readers have liked to be pushed aside as they were pushing aside the poor to favor the rich? Of course not. So James urged on them the "royal law": self-love as a measure of other-love. That's the way to avoid breaking God's Law.
   • Think of all the different situations in which you participate with other members of your church—attending worship, singing in the choir, studying in a home fellowship group, and so on. Now name some specific ways you can practice the "royal law" in those contexts.
   • Favoritism is a sin just like any other—a violation of God's Law. In a minute or two of silence, search your conscience for instances in your past when you showed favoritism, and then seek God's forgiveness for it.

3. As a motivation to be kinder to the poor (and a powerful motivation it is!), James informed his readers that they would receive mercy from God only as they had shown mercy to others.
   • What is "the law of liberty"? How does being judged by this law differ from being judged on the basis of obedience to Old Testament regulations?
   • What tends to keep Christians from being more generous in showing mercy?

4. A professed faith and a demonstrated faith are not necessarily the same thing. In fact, "faith" without an observable working out in real life is no faith at all.
   • Form a pair with someone sitting next to you and turn with your partner to the first item in "Bringing It Home" for day 4. One of you be "You" and the other "John" (or "Jean"), then switch, so that each of you gets to argue why a real faith is an acted-out faith.
   • In the last thirty days, what have you done (note: done, not said) that might lead an observer to conclude you're a Christian?

5. A faith without works is a faith without life. Abraham and Rahab are examples of people who were justified (in the sense of being proved righteous) by their works.
   • Divide into two groups. One group should find some way to creatively present the story of Abraham's near-sacrifice of Isaac (use your imagination—skit, radio drama, cartoon strip, puppet show, rap?), while the other group should do the same for Rahab's protection of the Hebrew spies. Present your stories to each other.
   • If you're troubled because it still sounds to you as though James was saying that salvation comes through works, ask for help from the others to understand James 2

better. Don't leave without a clear understanding of the difference between works
as a means of salvation and works as a
proof of salvation.
• Pick one tangible way that you are going
to show that your faith is alive during the
coming week. Ask a partner to hold you
accountable to do it.

Close your session in prayer, asking God to
help each one behave with selfless love
toward all and with tangible expressions of
mercy to the needy.

INTRODUCTION TO UNIT 3
WISDOM IN TAMING THE TONGUE (JAMES 3)

Destination: To understand that our speech is an evidence of the kind of wisdom we have embraced in our lives.

A story is told of a philosopher who planned to have guests for dinner. In preparation, he sent his servant to the market to purchase the best food he could find. When the guests arrived and were seated for the dinner, the servant brought out course after course of the same meat—tongue. Fried, baked, broiled, breaded, and plain, there was nothing to eat but tongue. The philosopher, obviously upset, demanded to know why the servant had brought home nothing but tongue when he had been instructed to get the best thing available in the market. The servant replied, "I did get the best thing in the market. Is not the tongue the organ of sociability, the organ of eloquence, the organ of kindness, the organ of worship?"

Stymied by this reply, the philosopher sent his servant back to the market the next day to procure the worst thing he could find. At the next meal, the philosopher sat down to exactly what he had been served before—tongue! Losing his patience by this time, the philosopher demanded to know why the servant had not brought the worst thing in the market as he had been instructed. "I did," the servant replied. "Is not the tongue the organ of blasphemy, the organ of defamation, the organ of boasting, the organ of lying?" (Adapted from Charles R. Swindoll, *The Tale of the Tardy Oxcart,* Word, 1998.)

One is tempted to wonder if the servant in this story was not the true philosopher. He certainly understood one thing—the double-edged nature of the tongue. Like the servant, James also understood the power of the tongue to accomplish both good and evil. In chapter 3 of his letter he warned his readers against the untamed nature of the tongue in its natural state. It is like the rudder that steers a ship or the spark that sets a forest ablaze—it is a tiny thing compared to the effect it can have.

But the tongue's impact is not always negative. Like the philosopher's servant said, the same organ can be a source of praise or prejudice, blasphemy or blessing. What makes the difference is the source of energy behind it. It's important to remember, when discussing the tongue, that we are talking about a fleshly muscle. Once, in teaching a Sunday school class on this portion of James, I (William) was going to go to the local farmer's market and purchase the largest beef tongue I could find (upward of a foot long). My goal was to take it to the class, flop it out on a table, and wait silently with the class for it to begin doing all the terrible things James said the (human) tongue will do. The point would then be obvious—the tongue, on its own, has no power at all. (Note: I didn't take the tongue; it seemed a bit too graphic. What do you think?)

Whether the tongue curses or cures is a function of the heart that directs it, and the heart is controlled by one of two sources of wisdom: heavenly or demonic. Wisdom learned from God is humble, peace-loving, considerate, submissive—James almost gave his own version of Paul's fruit of the Spirit. But devilish wisdom is earthly, bespeaking envy, selfishness, disorder, and all kinds of evil things. Parents used to wash out children's mouths to clean up their speech. But James would say, don't bother—it's the heart that needs cleaning.

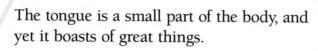 The tongue is a small part of the body, and yet it boasts of great things.

JAMES 3:5

DAY 1

WHY TALKING IS A DANGEROUS PRACTICE

At first glance, James 3 seems to have little to do with the first two chapters, but a closer look reveals that it is a specific application of the needed unity between faith and works. Picking up on something he mentioned in 1:19 and 1:26, James here offered a thorough treatment of the greatest danger facing his fellow Christian Jews—their own tongues. Speech is perhaps the clearest indicator of moral and spiritual character.

Interestingly, James cautioned those who would be teachers among the Jewish believers to think twice before becoming one. And he gave two reasons for this thinking twice: First, it's a given that you're going to stumble (say something you shouldn't have) when you teach; everyone who talks does.[98] Second, if you teach, you will be held accountable at a higher level because of the influence you have on others.[99] Therefore, he reasoned, don't rush to judgment (your own) by rushing to be a teacher.

THE DANGER IN TEACHING

Here's a bird's-eye view of teaching in the Bible that sheds some light on James' concern about the rush to teach in the early church: The various forms of the verb "teach," and the noun "teacher," occur (in English) more than 325 times in the Bible. About one-third of those occur in the Old Testament, two-thirds in the New Testament. Given the fact that the Old Testament comprises two-thirds of the Bible and the New Testament one-third, we have a reversal of occurrences. Purely on the basis of size, we would have expected teaching to be mentioned more in the Old Testament.

But if you think about the dynamics of both periods, you see why teaching is a hot topic in the New Testament. In the Old Testament, all the "knowledge" was given first to Moses, who wrote it down and passed it on to others. Things were codified and precise, leaving very little room for conjecture or interpretation. Therefore, teaching was the equivalent of reading with some marginal explanations.[T38] Ezra was an example of an Old Testament teacher.[100]

However, the New Testament era represented a time of massive change in Israel. Almost as a wordplay, the truth as it was given as a stewardship to the apostle Paul was being

---

[98]**JAMES 3**

2 We all stumble in many ways. If anyone does not stumble in what he says, he is a perfect man, able to bridle the whole body as well.

[99]**JAMES 3**

1 Let not many of you become teachers, my brethren, knowing that as such we will incur a stricter judgment.

[100]**EZRA 7**

10 Ezra had set his heart to study the law of the Lord and to practice it, and to teach His statutes and ordinances in Israel.

[101]**1 TIMOTHY 1**

3,7 As I urged you upon my departure for Macedonia, remain on at Ephesus so that you may instruct certain men not to teach strange doctrines. . . . [They want] to be teachers of the Law, even though they do not understand either what they are saying or the matters about which they make confident assertions.

[102]**LUKE 12**

48 "From everyone who has been given much, much will be required; and to whom they entrusted much, of him they will ask all the more."

[103]**ROMANS 3; 9**

3:2 [The Jews] were entrusted with the oracles of God.

9:3-5 . . . my kinsmen according to the flesh, who are Israelites, to whom belongs the adoption as sons, and the glory and the covenants and the giving of the Law and the temple service and the promises, whose are the fathers, and from whom is the Christ according to the flesh, who is over all, God blessed forever. Amen.

---

called a "mystery which had been kept secret for long ages past" (Romans 16:25). It wasn't just a mystery—it was a "great" mystery (Ephesians 5:32) that had been "hidden from the past ages and generations" (Colossians 1:26).[T39] As you might expect, the opportunity to be an expert on the mystery, to be a fount of authority and wisdom, was too great a temptation for many people to pass up. Lots of people wanted to be the next Ezra.[101]

Given that background, why do you think there are twice as many references to teaching in the New Testament as in the Old Testament?

But why will teachers "incur a stricter judgment"?[99] What insight does the principle stated by Jesus in Luke 12:48 offer to this question?[102]

What had been given to the leaders in Israel (see Romans 3:2; 9:3-5)?[103]

Instead of leading people into spiritual freedom with what they had been given, what had the Jewish leaders done?[104, T40]

Teaching is a weighty responsibility for many reasons, not the least of which is that people's eternal destiny can hinge on what they are taught. This is one of the reasons Jesus condemned the teachers of the Law in Israel. They had become "blind guides of the blind" (Matthew 15:14), failing to enter the kingdom of God themselves and keeping others from entering as well (Luke 11:52).

THE DANGER IN TALKING

Though James' words about teachers may have been prompted by some specific event unknown to us, don't ignore him just because you've never wanted to be a formal teacher. The truth is, everyone teaches someone. Think of your network of acquaintances—family, friends, work,

HISTORY & CULTURE:[T38]

TEACHING AS READING—
When the Israelites returned from seventy years of captivity in Babylon and began rebuilding the walls and city of Jerusalem, they needed to be taught the Word of God. A whole new generation of Israelites had grown up in Babylon without systematic instruction from Scripture. Therefore, Ezra the scribe was called on to read and expound the Law of Moses. For five to six hours, the people stood as Ezra read the Scriptures, which were later expounded by various Levites, "translating to give the sense so that they understood the reading" (Nehemiah 8:1-8). This pattern continues in evangelical churches today under the name of "expository preaching"—reading the text of Scripture and explaining its meaning. While James' warnings to teachers still apply today, they were all the more apropos at the time before the writing of the New Testament.

CROSS REFERENCES:[T39]

PAUL'S MYSTERY—The clearest statement of the mystery that had been hidden in the Old Testament and revealed to Paul is found in Ephesians 3:1-13, concisely summarized in verse 6: "The Gentiles are fellow heirs and fellow members of the body, and fellow partakers of the promise in Christ Jesus through the gospel." It had always been God's intent to bring salvation to the Gentiles (the Gentiles are the human race minus the Jews) through the Jewish people (Isaiah 42:6; 49:6; 60:3; Luke 2:32; Acts 13:47; 26:23). But it had not been revealed that God would combine Jews and Gentiles together into one new body, the church. This was what was revealed to Paul, and what he considered a stewardship from God (1 Corinthians 9:17; Ephesians 3:2; Colossians 1:25).

[104]**LUKE 20**

45-47 While all the people were listening, [Jesus] said to the disciples, "Beware of the scribes, who like to walk around in long robes, and love respectful greetings in the market places, and chief seats in the synagogues and places of honor at banquets, who devour widows' houses, and for appearance's sake offer long prayers. These will receive greater condemnation."

[105]**PROVERBS 3; 6; 13**

3:1-2 My son, do not forget my teaching, but let your heart keep my commandments; for length of days and years of life and peace they will add to you.

6:23 The commandment is a lamp and the teaching is light; and reproofs for discipline are the way of life.

13:14 The teaching of the wise is a fountain of life, to turn aside from the snares of death.

neighbors, church—and list all the people who, on some occasion, you teach (by "teach," we mean meeting a need by imparting skill or knowledge).

While you probably don't have a formal title of "teacher,"[T41] with most of those people, the same danger applies as to James' formal teachers: a probability of misspeaking (and the resulting accountability for what you say).

In order to point out the extreme danger of opening one's mouth, James made a profound statement: Anyone who can control his speech will be able to control the rest of his body.[98] We can take James' words one of two ways:

- Literally: If we are having a problem with sin in any area of our life, we should pray for our speech. Somehow, not sinning in speech will eradicate all other sin from our life.

- Figuratively: James was pointing out the explosive and powerful nature of the tongue and the difficulty we have in controlling it.

State some arguments to support both of these views.

- The literal view (hint: think in terms of self-discipline; if you are disciplined enough not to sin in speech, might you also be disciplined in other areas?):

- The figurative view (hint: look ahead to the next few verses):

BRINGING IT HOME

1. Have you ever been, or are you currently, in a formal position of teaching (either in a Christian or secular setting)? How do James' words influence your thinking on matters such as lesson preparation?

2. What is the difference between "talking" and "teaching" in terms of anticipated outcome? How do you know when you have truly taught someone?

3. James' words are true: "We all stumble in many ways" (James 3:2), especially when we talk. How many times have you finished a time of Bible reading or prayer, and a few minutes later had a sharp word for a family member? Or how about the proverbial case of the family riding to church firing audible artillery at each other before going inside to praise the Lord? Have you spoken a hurtful word recently? Decide today to make amends for it and restore the relationship that was damaged.

POINT OF INTEREST:[T40]

WOE TO TEACHERS—James 3:1 presents a microcosm of what James' half brother, Jesus Christ, taught on the subject of the Jewish religious teachers. These teachers (scribes) are mentioned nine times in Matthew 23, where Jesus pronounced seven "woes" upon them. Why? Because they did not practice what they preached. Eugene Peterson, in *The Message,* describes them this way: "You won't go wrong in following their teachings on Moses. But be careful about following *them.* They talk a good line, but they don't live it. They don't take it into their hearts and live it out in their behavior. It's all spit-and-polish veneer" (Matthew 23:3).

POINT OF INTEREST:[T41]

TEACHERS—In the New Testament there are two kinds of teachers: those who are called by God, and those who call themselves. The ones called by God are gifted with the spiritual gift of teaching (Romans 12:7; 1 Corinthians 12:28). Those with the gift of teaching were probably intended to be recognized as "teachers" (akin to an office) in the church (see Ephesians 4:11, where teaching is part of a hyphenated gift, or office, of pastor-teacher). On the other hand, it was apparently a task of leadership in the church to keep unqualified people from teaching (those who want to teach but are not gifted to do so). Allowing immature people to influence the church has dual liabilities: leading the flock astray and conceit (1 Timothy 3:6).

DAILY READING

Read Proverbs 3:1-2, 6:23, and 13:14.[105] Meditate on the power of sound teaching for those who receive and apply it.

106JEREMIAH 17

9 The heart is more deceitful than all else and is desperately sick; who can understand it?

107JAMES 3

3 If we put the bits into the horses' mouths so that they will obey us, we direct their entire body as well.

108JAMES 3

4 Look at the ships . . . , though they are so great and are driven by strong winds, are still directed by a very small rudder wherever the inclination of the pilot desires.

109JAMES 3

5 The tongue is a small part of the body, and yet it boasts of great things.

110PROVERBS 12

13-14 An evil man is ensnared by the transgression of his lips, but the righteous will escape from trouble. A man will be satisfied with good by the fruit of his words, and the deeds of a man's hands will return to him.

DAY 2

WHY THE TONGUE IS A DANGEROUS ORGAN

Sometimes it helps to read the end of the story first—to keep surprising details in perspective as you move along. Such is the case with James' final position about the tongue, the power of speech. Knowing and understanding his bottom line will make some of his rather dramatic statements a little less shocking.

In verses 7 and 8 we find what James believed about the tongue: "Every species of beasts and birds, of reptiles and creatures of the sea, is tamed and has been tamed by the human race. But no one can tame the tongue; it is a restless evil and full of deadly poison."

The reason the tongue can't be tamed (you won't ever see one in a cage at the zoo) is because it is not an independent entity. Speech doesn't just erupt out of the mouth; the tongue and vocal cords are moved into action by the human heart (mind, will, and emotions). In fact, the tongue is so passive in and of itself that we can say the tongue is simply a mirror of the heart. Can't see what is in your own heart or the heart of another person? Not to worry. Given enough time, you'll hear it with your own ears.

Given the prophet Jeremiah's perspective on the natural condition of the human heart,[106] what are the chances of a person "taming" the heart in order to tame the tongue?

If the tongue can't be tamed without taming the heart, and if the heart itself is untamable, we have a dilemma. Only by embracing heavenly wisdom can the works of one's tongue be consistent with one's faith. James supplied this solution at the end of chapter 3. For now, let's group James' words in verses 3-7 into three different analogies that will help us see how he arrived at his conclusion in verse 8.

THE ANALOGY OF PROPORTION

Proportional relationships help us and surprise us. They help us in math and mapmaking to produce small models of large things. And they surprise us at times when we see the effect of something relative to its size.[T42] James said that the power and influence of the tongue (human speech) is out of proportion to its size.

Cite the two illustrations James offered of small things that influence the direction of larger things:

• James 3:3[107]

• James 3:4[108]

Completing the analogy from proportion, what large result can emanate from a small organ like the tongue (verse 5)?[109]

It's important to note that, at this point, James made no comment about positive or negative results. He only noted the power of a small thing to control a large one. Can you cite an example of how a horse's bridle, a ship's rudder, and the tongue can be used with both positive and negative results?

	Positive	Negative
Horse's bridle		
Ship's rudder		
The tongue		

Supply the correct word (small, large) to complete this summary statement:

For good or for ill, the impact of the _____ thing is a function of who is controlling the _____ thing.

THE ANALOGY OF PROVERBS

By focusing attention on the power of speech, James paralleled a priority in the Old Testament book of Proverbs. Record the truths about speech revealed in the following proverbs:[T43]

POINT OF INTEREST:[T42]
ALBERT EINSTEIN—Humanly speaking, Albert Einstein was a man who had a disproportional impact on our world during his lifetime. One major poll at the end of 1999 even named him "Man of the Century." Not only was he small in stature, but he studied small things that ended up radically changing the world. His studies of molecules, atoms, and energy led him (along with other scientists) to write a letter to President Franklin Roosevelt in 1939 proposing the possibility of an atomic bomb. The resulting development of nuclear energy has changed human existence—both positively and negatively—like no other discovery. And consider Einstein's most famous mathematical formula, $E=mc^2$. This formula, expressing his theory of relativity, is probably the smallest thing defining a "largest" thing ever conceived. His theory of relativity unlocked previously hidden relationships about space and time in the universe.

[111]**PROVERBS 12**
18 There is one who speaks rashly like the thrusts of a sword, but the tongue of the wise brings healing.

[112]**PROVERBS 13**
14 The teaching of the wise is a fountain of life, to turn aside the snares of death.

[113]**PROVERBS 16**
24 Pleasant words are a honeycomb, sweet to the soul and healing to the bones.

[114]**PROVERBS 16**
27 A worthless man digs up evil, while his words are like scorching fire.

[115]**PROVERBS 18**
21 Death and life are in the power of the tongue, and those who love it will eat its fruit.

[116]**PROVERBS 25**
18 Like a club and a sword and a sharp arrow is a man who bears false witness against his neighbor.

[117]**JAMES 3**
5-6,8 See how great a forest is set aflame by such a small fire! And the tongue is a fire, the very world of iniquity; the tongue is set among our members as that which defiles the entire body, and sets on fire the course of our life, and is set on fire by hell. . . .

But no one can tame the tongue; it is a restless evil and full of deadly poison.

- Proverbs 12:13-14[110]

- Proverbs 12:18[111]

- Proverbs 13:14[112] (see also 10:11)

- Proverbs 16:24[113]

- Proverbs 16:27[114]

- Proverbs 18:21[115]

- Proverbs 25:18[116]

THE ANALOGY OF POTENTIAL

James cited two natural phenomena to show the potential of the tongue: fire and poison.[117] When we think of forest fires, we think of the destruction of multitudes of living things: trees, plants, and animals. When we think of poisons, however, our mind goes first to harm brought to an individual—a baby poisoned by a household cleaning product, a hiker poisoned by a venomous snake bite, a person poisoned by contaminated food.

Following that train of thought, describe how the tongue, like fire, could have a destructive impact on multitudes of people at one time.

Then describe how the tongue, like poison, could be used to destroy the life or reputation of a single individual.

Don't forget, fire (as in heat) is used to cook our food, and some poisons (like chlorine in our water and venom in vaccines) have positive impacts on our bodies. It all depends on who's in control!

BRINGING IT HOME

1. Describe an instance lately when your speech produced a positive result, and another time when the result was negative.

2. What made the difference? Were you in control of your tongue both times, or out of control?

3. Before going further, think back about the instance that turned out negatively. Do you need to repair any damage that resulted in a relationship or other situation? If so, determine to correct the negative impact of your speech as soon as possible. Make a phone call, write a letter, pay a visit—whatever it takes. Remember, fire and poison are at work until they are removed by a stronger force (in this case, you).

LANGUAGE & LIT:[T43]

BLUE-COLLAR THEOLOGY— James is often thought of as the workingman's theologian because he expressed truth in the workaday language of the street. While the apostle Paul gave us the sophisticated theology of the academy (which we need), James stuck to his get-a-bigger-hammer approach of the Old Testament. Remember, the book of James is all about wisdom, how to be skilled at the job of living. It sounds like Proverbs because that's the kind of book Proverbs is: a book that can be used by non-Christians as well as Christians. When you get a new appliance nowadays, the instructions will be in several modern languages. But there isn't a set for Christians and non-Christians. Why? Because you don't have to be spiritual to push the On button and make it work. Proverbs and James are like that. They just want you to understand this thing called life and find the On buttons that will allow you to live it successfully.

DAILY READING

Read Isaiah 55:10-11.[44] Consider what your recent words have accomplished in the lives of those to whom they were spoken.

DAY 3

THE SOURCE OF SPEECH

Grade-B western movies always had the Native American characters referring to the bad guy as someone who "speaks with forked tongue." That's not a bad way to describe someone whose tongue produces truth one day and lies the next. James would probably have agreed with that metaphor to describe the person he had in mind when writing the next verses of his letter—the person who speaks spiritually in one breath and carnally in the next. James was still on a mission to reveal the inconsistency, even the hypocrisy, of Christians claiming to have faith and yet living as if they don't, especially when it comes to the tongue.

We noted in the last lesson that the tongue does not work independently of the heart. Here James used images from nature, especially that of a spring from which water flows, to illustrate how inconsistent speech represents a divided heart (which reminds us of his "double-minded man" in 1:8). His words about speech quickly call to mind the words of his elder half brother, Jesus, who spoke on the same subject using metaphors from nature as well:

> "Each tree is known by its own fruit. For men do not gather figs from thorns, nor do they pick grapes from a briar bush. The good man out of the good treasure of his heart brings forth what is good; and the evil man out of the evil treasure brings forth what is evil; *for his mouth speaks from that which fills his heart*." (Luke 6:44-45, emphasis added)

THE PROBLEM WITH INCONSISTENT SPEECH

If we read only verse 10 of James 3, it would be easy to think that James was focusing simply on the inconsistency of using harsh language when speaking to or about a person while using the language of praise when speaking to and about God. And that certainly is inconsistent. On the basis of verse 10 alone, what is inconsistent about this kind of behavior?[118]

Sidebar references

[118]JAMES 3

10 From the same mouth come both blessing and cursing. My brethren, these things ought not to be this way.

[119]COLOSSIANS 4

6 Let your speech always be with grace, as though seasoned with salt, so that you will know how you should respond to each person.

[120]COLOSSIANS 3

8-10 Put them all aside: anger, wrath, malice, slander, and abusive speech from your mouth. Do not lie to one another, since you laid aside the old self with its evil practices, and have put on the new self who is being renewed to a true knowledge according to the image of the One who created him.

[121]JAMES 3

9 With [the tongue] we bless our Lord and Father, and with it we curse men, who have been made in the likeness of God.

[122]GENESIS 9

5-6 "Surely I will require your lifeblood; from every beast I will require it. And from every man, from every man's brother I will require the life of man. Whoever sheds man's blood, by man his blood shall be shed, for in the image of God He made man."

What kind of speech did the apostle Paul suggest we use when talking to other people (Colossians 4:6)?[119] (What do you think "seasoned with salt" means?)

Paul explained, in more detail than James, *why* Christians should not speak in a manner inconsistent with their faith (Colossians 3:8-10).[120] What is the reason?

There is no question, on the basis of James 3:10 and the rest of Scripture, that the speech of a believer in Christ should manifest love and grace regardless of who one is talking to. But James was concerned about an even deeper inconsistency—one that is more serious than just using inappropriate language. He was concerned about Christians cursing[T44] (speaking with ill will toward, suggesting harmful results for) someone who bears the image of God![121, T45]

When God created man and woman, He created them in His own image and likeness (Genesis 1:26-27). The image of God distinguished humans from animals and allowed communication and fellowship between the Creator and the highest part of His creation, humankind (Psalm 8:3-9). Because human beings bear the image of God, they represent creation's highest worth. How was this explained to Noah after the Flood?[122]

James called the image of God "the likeness of God."[121] Explain why it is inconsistent to praise God but curse someone made in the image of God (remember, the image of God is in many ways a "representation" of God on earth).

Paul added even another layer of inconsistency in Colossians 3:10.[120] He said believers are being renewed "according to the image of the One" who created us. So we

LANGUAGE & LIT:[T44]

IMPRECATORY LANGUAGE— James' warning against believers calling out curses on others might seem to be in contradiction to frequent imprecations (curses) in Scripture. Numerous psalms (for example, Psalms 2, 37, 69, 79, 109, 139, and 143) contain prayers asking God to bring judgment against the enemies of the psalmist (who were also enemies of the work of God). New Testament passages contain imprecations as well (Luke 11:37-52; Galatians 1:8-9, Revelation 6:10; 18:20; 19:1-6). This type of literature can be justified because the requests are not self-centered but God-centered. They have God's righteous interests at heart; they are motivated by the same spirit in which Jesus cleansed the temple in Jerusalem. James' words warn against self-centered, vengeful language, not the language of imprecation.

CROSS REFERENCES:[T45]

THE IMAGE OF GOD—Many Scripture passages make reference to the fact that humans were created by God and in His image (Genesis 1:26-27; 5:1,3; 9:6; Psalm 8; Acts 17:22-31; 1 Corinthians 11:7; Ephesians 4:24; Colossians 3:10; James 3:9). While the words for "image" and "likeness" normally refer to the outward, visible form (1 Samuel 6:5; 2 Kings 16:10) of a copy, that is not the meaning of "image of God." Since God is spirit (John 4:24) and no one has seen God (John 1:18), it would be impossible to say that humans are a physical copy of God. Most theologians believe that the image of God in humans refers to intangibles such as personality, capacity for moral judgment, the sense of eternity, a conscience, and a developed ability to reason. These are the capacities that set humans apart from the rest of creation.

[123]JAMES 3

11-12 Does a fountain send out from the same opening both fresh and bitter water? Can a fig tree, my brethren, produce olives, or a vine produce figs? Nor can salt water produce fresh.

have believers who are in the image of God cursing others who are in the image of God—which approaches the ludicrous picture of God cursing Himself! There's obviously something wrong with this picture.

THE PURPOSE OF A CONSISTENT SOURCE

James' last two verses are meant to illustrate how people should evidence consistency just like the rest of creation.[123, T46] James intended to raise questions in his readers' minds about the true nature (rather than the supposed nature) of the source of their speech—the heart. Here's how he did it:

- Say we are on a hike and are directed to a nearby spring where we can replenish our water supply. We were told it is a freshwater spring, and there is a sign that says it is fresh water, yet when we sample the water, it is obviously salt water. What must we conclude about the true nature of the spring?

- If we grow hungry and are directed to a nearby fig tree but discover it has olives on it, what must we conclude about the kind of tree it is?

- What about a luscious grape arbor we see in the distance, but there find the vines full of a figlike fruit? Are we really looking at a grapevine?

- We meet a person who says he is a Christian, and who displays all the outward trappings of Christianity, but who spews forth speech that is full of curses toward his neighbors. What was James, by his use of analogies from nature, trying to get his readers to understand about the relationship of their speech to their true spiritual nature?

BRINGING IT HOME

1. Inappropriate speech can be manifested in different ways. Angry, even violent, outbursts of abusive language are not as common as another more controlled, but no less carnal, kind—gossip, hurtful or derogatory comments, lying, or prideful exaggeration. What part of your own speech patterns fails to reflect the image of God most consistently?

2. What do you do when you wound another by your speech or speak publicly in an inconsistent manner? How do you seek to make amends?

3. How could you use this portion of James to help a Christian friend who has a problem with his or her speech?

POINT OF INTEREST:[T46]

ARGUMENTS FROM NATURE—Scripture writers often used illustrations from nature to express God's truth. For instance, the existence of God is evident to all humans in the designs found in creation (Romans 1:19-20). Homosexual relationships are perversions of the two-gender relationships found throughout creation (Romans 1:26-27). And according to James, nature's sources do not support the idea of two opposing strains of words emanating from the same source. When we speak blasphemies instead of blessings, we call into question the true nature of the source of the words.

DAILY READING

Read Ecclesiastes 5:1-7 (see appendix A). Mark warnings against inconsistency found in this passage.

DAY 4

THE FOOLISHNESS OF EARTHLY "WISDOM"

The Bible is filled with contrasts—extremes at opposite ends of a spectrum of truth that help to illuminate and reveal what is in between. We read of darkness and light, the first Adam and the last Adam (Christ), law and grace, death and life, hell and heaven. While the positions at either end of the spectrum are positions of truth (there is a real heaven and a real hell), life for us is lived more on the continuum. Though Christians are children of light, we still encounter darkness in our lives. While we are saved by grace, we still do battle against the law of sin and death.

James gave us another set of contrasts in verses 13-18 of chapter 3: the contrast between earthly "wisdom" and heavenly wisdom. And like other contrasts, while our lives are based on heavenly wisdom, we sometimes find ourselves muddling around in the middle—wise today, foolish tomorrow. James apparently had gotten word that some believers in the dispersed church were more than occasionally unwise. Their lives were becoming characterized by a devilish sort of wisdom that was creating significant problems. In this lesson we will look at their foolish behavior (earthly "wisdom") and its result. In the next lesson we'll see James' remedy for their foolishness.

SO YOU THINK YOU'RE WISE?

James' summary statement in verse 13[124] is consistent with the message of his letter so far: Christians must live what they say they believe. If they do not, then their "faith" is more profession than possession; it may not be saving faith at all.

It appears he may still have been addressing those who wanted to become teachers in their churches,[99] as he called them the "wise" and "understanding."[T47] Describe in your own words, using verse 13, who is qualified to be a teacher (that is, who is truly wise and understanding).

Without suggesting that reputation is a goal to pursue (reputations happen naturally), it needs to be said that

---

13 Who among you is wise and understanding? Let him show by his good behavior his deeds in the gentleness of wisdom.

125 1 KINGS 3
28 When all Israel heard of the judgment which the king had handed down, they feared the king, for they saw that the wisdom of God was in him to administer justice.

126 1 KINGS 11
41 Now the rest of the acts of Solomon and whatever he did, and his wisdom, are they not written in the book of the acts of Solomon?

127 1 KINGS 10
23-24 King Solomon became greater than all the kings of the earth in riches and in wisdom. All the earth was seeking the presence of Solomon, to hear his wisdom which God had put in his heart.

truly wise and understanding people demonstrate their wisdom and understanding in a way that others can see. They don't try to demonstrate it; they don't seek to impress with it; it just happens in the normal course of events. This is what James was saying—if you would *be* wise and understanding (if you want to be known as being a teacher, a wise and understanding person), then be wise and understanding.

For instance, read the story in 1 Kings 3:16-28 (see appendix A). What did Solomon *do* that demonstrated his wisdom?

Why were the people convinced he was wise (remember the word "skill" as you answer)?[125]

How many other things like this did Solomon apparently do?[126]

What kind of reputation did Solomon eventually develop?[127]

Read Matthew 9:1-7[128] and describe how Jesus proved His "talk" by His "walk."

STUDY TECHNIQUES:[T47]

WISDOM AND UNDERSTANDING—We can gain wisdom and understanding in our study of Scripture through the use of computerized study aids. For instance, James mentioned wisdom and understanding together in the same verse (James 3:13). We know James had his roots in the Old Testament wisdom literature, and that "wisdom" and "understanding" are both words that occur in Proverbs. But is there more here? What about the phrase "wisdom and understanding"? Did James choose to link these two words together based on his Old Testament heritage? To find out using traditional means, we would have to look up "wisdom" in a standard concordance, then "understanding," and see if we could correlate the verses where both words appear. But with a computerized concordance, in an instant we are presented with all the verses in the Bible that contain both words. And it so happens that there are 43 of them in the Old Testament and only three in the New Testament (based on the *New American Standard* translation). There appears to be a trend!

Upon examining the Old Testament verses, we discover that "wisdom and understanding" was a Hebraism for an unusual depth of knowledge, prowess, and skill. The words are used as synonyms, often in parallelisms, to complement one another. And it becomes obvious why James, given his Hebrew background, used them together to describe those who wanted to be known as learned and profound in the faith. His Jewish readers would have understood immediately what takes us a few mouse clicks to discover. But the effort is well worth it and gives us greater understanding of his letter.

[128]**MATTHEW 9**

1-7 Getting into a boat, Jesus crossed over the sea and came to His own city. And they brought to Him a paralytic lying on a bed. Seeing their faith, Jesus said to the paralytic, "Take courage, son; your sins are forgiven." And some of the scribes said to themselves, "This fellow blasphemes." And Jesus knowing their thoughts said, "Why are you thinking evil in your hearts? Which is easier, to say, 'Your sins are forgiven,' or to say, 'Get up, and walk'? But so that you may know that the Son of Man has authority on earth to forgive sins"—then He said to the paralytic, "Get up, pick up your bed and go home." And he got up and went home.

[129]**MATTHEW 9**

8 When the crowds saw this, they were awestruck, and glorified God, who had given such authority to men.

[130]**MATTHEW 7**

29 [Jesus] was teaching them as one having authority, and not as their scribes.

[131]**JAMES 3**

14-15 If you have bitter jealousy and selfish ambition in your heart, do not be arrogant and so lie against the truth. This wisdom is not that which comes down from above, but is earthly, natural, demonic.

[132]**JAMES 3**

16 Where jealousy and selfish ambition exist, there is disorder and every evil thing.

Compare the response of the people to Jesus[129] and Solomon[125] with what people were used to seeing and hearing from their scribes in Jesus' day.[130]

Regarding the people James was addressing in verse 13 of chapter 3[124], who were they acting more like: Jesus and Solomon, or the scribes? How can you tell?

EARTHLY "WISDOM"

If, as we've suggested earlier in our study, we substitute the word "skill" for "wisdom," then "earthly skill" begins to make more sense. James was comparing skill sets, if you will—those of heaven and those of earth. Write down all the words in verses 14-15 that describe the way *not* to go about living your life as a Christian.[131]

It appears that this is how James' readers were living their lives. In fact, they appeared to be taking pride in their behavior (verse 14).[T48] But what was the net (negative) effect of their lifestyles?[T49]

Who was apparently influencing this behavior in the churches to whom James was writing (verse 15)?[131]

THE RESULTS OF EARTHLY "WISDOM"

What do the words "jealousy" (or "envy" in some translations) and "selfish ambition" suggest to you about the motivation of those James was addressing?[132]

Why is disorder always the result of environments where jealousy and selfish ambition are unchecked?

BRINGING IT HOME

1. If we asked people who know you well, how would they answer the following questions about you: To what degree does (your name) live what he/she believes? What gaps are there between his/her walk and talk?

2. What obstacles stand in the way of narrowing the gap? What would help you the most to overcome them?

3. It's important to understand that most Christians will never be in a place to demonstrate their "works" like Solomon and Jesus. Rather, our works will be shown in our homes, in our workplace, in our churches, and in relationships with friends and others. The key phrase in this passage that stands in contrast to "jealousy and self-ish ambition" is in verse 13: "the gentleness of wisdom." True wisdom is not arrogant or prideful; rather, it is strength under control (the Greek word for "gentle" was used to describe a powerful horse under the control of a bridle). Faith is proved genuine by gentle wisdom. When children see gentle wisdom in their mother or father, it is as astounding to them as Solomon's or Jesus' more public displays were to the crowds. So be encouraged! Whether you know it or not, someone is observing the gentleness of your wisdom in every situation—and being motivated by the faith that is behind it.

LANGUAGE & LIT:[T48]

NO "IFS" ABOUT IT—What appears to be a suggestion, or a hypothetical situation, in James 3:14 is actually a fact. By saying, "If . . ." James was not wondering whether the teachers he was talk-ing about were guilty of "bitter jealousy and selfish ambition." He was saying that they *were in fact* guilty. The Greek language had several ways in which "If . . ." could be written. It could imply "If (and you are) . . . ," "If (and you aren't) . . . ," or other possibilities. Here the Greek construction James used is "If (and you are) . . ." Those whom he addressed *were in fact* guilty of bitter jealousy and selfish ambition, and therefore of creating disorder in the church (verse 16).

LANGUAGE & LIT:[T49]

"AND" OR "OR"?—An important idea is at stake in James 3:14, and it is handled differently by two of the most popular modern transla-tions, the *New American Standard Bible* and the *New International Version*. The NASB says, "Do not be arrogant and so lie against the truth," while the NIV says, "Do not boast about it or deny the truth." The NASB has arrogance resulting in the truth being denied, while the NIV has arrogance and denying the truth as separate events. The NASB's translation is to be preferred, and it furnishes an important connection between our lifestyle and the truth we are seeking to proclaim. Those teachers James was addressing were denying the very truth they were trying to teach—denying it by their lives. How does my life vali-date or invalidate the truth I profess to believe?

DAILY READING

Read Luke 6:43-49 (see appendix A). Mark those words of Jesus that bear similarity to James' words.

DAY 5

THE GENTLENESS OF HEAVENLY WISDOM

[133] JAMES 3

17 The wisdom from above is first pure, then peaceable, gentle, reasonable, full of mercy and good fruits, unwavering, without hypocrisy.

[134] ROMANS 7

15 What I am doing, I do not understand; for I am not practicing what I would like to do, but I am doing the very thing I hate.

[135] ROMANS 7; 8

7:25 Thanks be to God through Jesus Christ our Lord! So then, on the one hand I myself with my mind am serving the law of God, but on the other, with my flesh the law of sin.

8:1 Therefore there is now no condemnation for those who are in Christ Jesus.

In the lesson for day 2 of this unit, we identified a dilemma. The tongue of the human species is "a restless evil and full of deadly poison" (James 3:8), unable to be tamed. The tongue is a mirror of the heart, itself a "deceitful" and "desperately sick" organ (Jeremiah 17:9). We have an untamable tongue controlled by a deceitful heart—why should we expect speech of any but a boastful and evil sort? We shouldn't, considering people in their natural state.

But James was not addressing the natural man or woman in his letter; he was addressing the church of Jesus Christ. And in these last verses of chapter 3, he described the only thing that can tame the untamable tongue: the gentle wisdom from heaven.[124] To understand what James meant, we have to remember who he was—that is, he was not the sophisticated theologian that Paul was. Paul was trained by Gamaliel; James, by his carpenter father, Joseph.[T50] Paul was an apostolic theologian; James, a pastor. When James wrote, he wrote in plain, big-idea concepts designed to help plain people be better believers. From James we get nothing about the filling and fruit of the Holy Spirit resulting in the self-control of the tongue. James' theology was not that refined.[T51] He had but one message for the church: To say heaven is your home, you must speak like a citizen of heaven, and to do that, you must embrace the wisdom that comes down from above.[133]

HEAVENLY WISDOM

James described in verses 14-16 the impact of living and talking using earthly wisdom. He did not paint a pretty picture, and yet we know from our own experience the damage that the tongue can cause. What he described is entirely consistent with his description of the power of the tongue in verses 5-8.

What has been your experience? The older we get, and the longer we have been a Christian, the more discouraged we can become over past and present manifestations of our heart via our speech. How do you feel about the current state of your speech, your ability to say what you want to say when you want to say it?[T52]

What do Paul's words in Romans 7:15[134] suggest to you about even an apostle's ability to always say the right thing?

What was Paul's solution to every area of failure in his life?[135]

The "heavenly wisdom" that James recommended[133] means availing ourselves of the help God offers to do that which we cannot do in our own nature and strength. Fill in the following chart as a way to summarize what James presented concerning earthly versus heavenly wisdom:

	Earthly Wisdom	Heavenly Wisdom
Source	1	2
	(3:15)	(3:17)
Motivation	3	4
	(3:14)	(3:17)"It is first . . ."
Manifestation	5	6
	(3:16)	(3:17)". . . then . . ."

Can you see where James was going? Remember, his overall goal in his letter was to help his readers live out what they said they believed. To see the inconsistency of their present behavior, look again at the chart above. Drawing a line connecting box 2 with box 5 just doesn't make sense, does it? Yet that's how some of James' readers were living—totally inconsistent with their stated beliefs. Or try starting with box 5 and drawing a line back to box 4. How can one be producing disorder with his life and claim pure motives?

How about your life? As a Christian, your starting point should be box 2. Where would a line illustrating your life go from there?

JEWISH EDUCATION—Three primary avenues existed for education following the return of the Jews from exile in Babylon. First and foundational, was the home. Jewish parents (see references to the words of both mothers and fathers in Proverbs) were responsible for teaching their children at home (Deuteronomy 6:1-9). Second was the synagogue, which as an institution probably arose during the exile and continued in Israel following the return of the exiles. The purpose of the synagogues was to expound the Law for the community and offer interpretations of its meaning (Luke 4:16-28). Both James and Paul probably benefited from training in the home and the synagogue, but Paul's training included a further level: attachment, as a disciple, to a learned rabbi for scholarly training in the Law. Paul was a student of Gamaliel (Acts 5:34-39; 22:3), who sat at the feet of Hillel, one of the two most revered rabbis in first-century Jerusalem. Paul's scholarly training becomes evident in his letters, as James' more earthy and home-based training is evident in his letter.

[136] **JAMES 3**

18 The seed whose fruit is righteousness is sown in peace by those who make peace.

[137] **ROMANS 14**

17 The kingdom of God is not eating and drinking, but righteousness and peace and joy in the Holy Spirit.

[138] **LUKE 16**

13 "No servant can serve two masters; for either he will hate the one and love the other, or else he will be devoted to one and despise the other. You cannot serve God and wealth."

RESULTS OF HEAVENLY WISDOM

Not surprisingly, Proverbs offers a striking comparison between those whose motivation is characterized by deceit (resulting in evil) and those whose motivation is peace (resulting in joy). "Deceit is in the heart of those who devise evil, but counselors of peace have joy" (Proverbs 12:20). What did James say is the result of embracing heavenly wisdom as a way of life?[136]

What was James contrasting righteousness with (verse 16)?[132]

What are joy, righteousness, and peace all characteristics of?[137]

Seeing this verse from Romans helps to bring James' big idea into focus even more clearly. He was talking about a conflict in the church (in the believer's life) between the kingdom (values) of God and the kingdom (values) of the Devil (3:15). What did Jesus say about trying to serve two competing sets of values at the same time?[138]

BRINGING IT HOME

1. What has meant the most to you as you have studied James 3 this week?

Things That Have Been Confirmed for Me:	Things That Were Surprises or Challenges for Me:

2. From today's study, have you sensed conflicting sets of values in your life as a Christian in the area of your speech (source, motives, manifestation)?

   Have you sensed conflicting sets of values in any other area of your life besides speech (motives or manifestations not consistent with kingdom values)?

3. Write out a brief prayer to God concerning the most important change needed in your life as a result of any of this week's studies.

STUDY TECHNIQUES:[T51]

READING GOD'S BOOK—Here are things to remember when studying God's Word: (1) The people who wrote it did not know they were writing a book that looks like our Bible. They were simply addressing real issues at the time in which they lived. (2) The authors were human beings of a multitude of sorts. They were scholars, shepherds, fishermen, and tradesmen of all sorts, and they wrote out of their human conditions. (3) The Holy Spirit inspired and guided all the writing (2 Timothy 3:16; 2 Peter 1:21), producing inerrant truth from the perspective of the individual authors. (4) The most helpful way to study the Bible is to read *all* of it in a complementary fashion. One of the greatest evidences of the inspiration of Scripture is how the authors complement, rather than contradict, one another.

POINT OF INTEREST:[T52]

THE OLDER I GET . . .—Older Christians can grow discouraged when they struggle with sin—but they shouldn't. Nowhere does the Bible say we will be perfect in this life—only better (and when we think our "better" isn't good enough, it's often because we don't realize exactly how far we had fallen to begin with). Besides, the more we see of Jesus and His righteousness, the clearer our sin becomes. Peter probably wouldn't have wept over denying Jesus after knowing Him for three days, but he did weep after knowing Him for three years. Be encouraged about the changes in your speech you have seen—and thankful that God has allowed you to care deeply about that part of your life!

DAILY READING

Read Galatians 5:16-26 (see appendix A). Note the comparison of two competing worldviews, much as James presented in the last part of James 3.

To the leader: Bring enough flower seeds to the session so that each member of the group can have a few. Perhaps you can even provide starter pots.

1. James forced his readers to count the cost if they wanted to become teachers: Teachers are held to a higher standard of responsibility as speakers with authority. And yet, maintaining control over one's speech is hard for everybody.
   - Which describes you better: Martin Motormouth, Zelda Zip-Lip, or Prudence Prudent-Speech?
   - In what sense(s) are you a "teacher"? Why do you think teachers incur a stricter judgment? Does this seem fair to you? Why or why not?
   - Tell about an occasion when you said something you shouldn't have. What were the ramifications for you and for others? Why is it so hard to keep from saying the wrong thing?

2. The tongue is a small part of the body, yet it boasts of big things. Furthermore, it can do much damage.
   - James used the metaphors of a ship's rudder and a horse's bit to picture how the small tongue has a large, controlling influence. Name some modern metaphors for the same thing (for example, a steering wheel directs an entire automobile).
   - If someone were to assert that James was exaggerating when he said the tongue is "set on fire by hell" (James 3:9), how would you reply?
   - Have you ever been "poisoned" by someone else's tongue? Describe the experience.

3. Christians use their tongues both to bless the Lord and to curse people. But this is wrong. It should be considered unnatural.

- In what ways do Christians sometimes "curse" people, that is, speak with ill will toward or about them? (Think of subtle as well as obvious ways.)
- Wes has a problem with his speech. He often complains about his boss to his coworkers. When he gets together with his older brother, they slip back into their childish pattern of insulting each other. Perhaps out of a sense of inferiority, Wes tends to belittle others to make himself look bigger. Yet Wes is a Christian who sings the praise of God every Sunday morning and Wednesday night!
  If Wes came to you for advice on how to retrain his tongue so that he only blesses, never curses, what would you recommend?

4. Those who wish to be considered wise and understanding should act that way. They should rely on gentle, godly wisdom and not be motivated by ambition and jealousy.
   - Who exemplifies for you "the gentleness of wisdom" (James 3:13), and why?
   - If someone wanted to be considered wise (skillful, expert) merely out of ambition and envy of others, how could you detect the misguided motivation?

5. Heavenly wisdom is filled with all kinds of fine and sweet qualities. And from it grows righteousness in a bed of peace.
   - Going around the circle, each person should take one of the qualities of heavenly wisdom in verse 17 and complete the sentence "Heavenly wisdom is pure in that it is . . ." or "Heavenly wisdom is peaceable in that it is . . ." and so on. (The other qualities are "gentle," "reasonable," "full of mercy," "full of good fruits," "unwavering," and "without hypocrisy.")
   - Set a goal for yourself to begin living by holy wisdom in your speech. Take a few

seeds home with you and use them to raise a flower that will remind you of your new determination.

As everyone is holding his or her seeds, pray a prayer of commitment to follow through on your goals. Then bless the Lord by singing together a verse of a favorite praise hymn or chorus.

INTRODUCTION TO UNIT 4
WISDOM FOR THE HUMBLE AND THE HOPEFUL (JAMES 4)

Destination: To learn that the correct approach to achieving present and future goals is to live in humility before God.

The first job I (William) took after graduating from seminary was teaching seventh and eighth grade Bible classes in a large Christian school. Having already earned another graduate degree prior to spending four years in seminary, I felt I was prepared for something more "challenging"—but God knew better. As the teaching year wore on, I became increasingly frustrated with my lot in life. Married with two young children and a third on the way, our months routinely outlasted our money. I helped coach the football team to add extra income to our salary, but still we were barely getting by. The large church that sponsored the school had a counselor on staff who I went to see for "advice" about my situation (actually, I went to whine).

Our conversation was brief, beginning like this: I explained my background (he wasn't impressed), our financial pressures (he wasn't sympathetic), and my question ("Why doesn't the school pay its teachers more?"). Here's how it ended: "William, were the terms of the job explained clearly to you when you were hired?"

"Yes, they were."

"Was there mutual agreement that it was the Lord's will for you to take the job?"

"Yes, there was."

"Then I think the frustration you are experiencing is of your own making. Perhaps the school should pay its teachers more, but that's really not the issue. The issue is your willingness to humble yourself before the Lord, who you believe led you here, and before the students and administration, who you agreed to serve. It may not be the Lord's will for you to teach here next year. But for this year, I believe your joy will return when you submit yourself to the plan and provision God has for you and your family at the present time."

Ouch! That wasn't what I wanted to hear. But it was the truth and therefore what I needed. And though that conversation happened more than twenty years ago, I have never forgotten it. God used an older, wiser man to teach me that neither my present nor my future circumstances are the key to joy in life, and neither are they of primary concern to God. What is of most concern to Him is my character, specifically my willingness to exchange pride for humility.

James knew the believers to whom he wrote needed to learn the same lesson. And the same is true of his readers today. Pride—thinking more highly of ourselves than we ought to think—undoubtedly stands at the heart of almost all human conflict. Because pride manifests itself in a number of different ways, all of which seem entirely justifiable at the moment, it is sometimes hard to detect. We become so convinced that we are right in what we are pursuing that we fail to see what God may want to accomplish through our circumstances. We become so entrenched in our pride, James indicated, that we attract the Devil himself, and the only way to cause him to flee is to submit ourselves once again to God (James 4:7).

Chapter 4 of James is all about the trouble that pride causes in our present and in our plans for the future. Learning humility doesn't ensure a larger salary or a more prestigious calling, but it does lead to something far more important: the development of kingdom virtues and values in our character.

 God is opposed to the proud, but gives grace to the humble.

JAMES 4:6

[139] **JAMES 4**

6 GOD IS OPPOSED TO THE PROUD, BUT GIVES GRACE TO THE HUMBLE.

[140] **JAMES 4**

2 You lust and do not have; so you commit murder. You are envious and cannot obtain; so you fight and quarrel. You do not have because you do not ask.

[141] **JAMES 4**

1 What is the source of quarrels and conflicts among you? Is not the source your pleasures that wage war in your members?

[142] **ISAIAH 14**

13-14 You said in your heart, "I will ascend to heaven; I will raise my throne above the stars of God, and I will sit on the mount of assembly in the recesses of the north. I will ascend above the heights of the clouds; I will make myself like the Most High."

[143] **MATTHEW 5**

21-22 "You have heard that the ancients were told, 'YOU SHALL NOT COMMIT MURDER' and 'Whoever commits murder shall be liable to the court.' But I say to you that everyone who is angry with his brother shall be guilty before the court; and whoever says to his brother, 'You good-for-nothing,' shall be guilty before the supreme court; and whoever says, 'You fool,' shall be guilty enough to go into the fiery hell."

[144] **1 JOHN 3**

15 Everyone who hates his brother is a murderer; and you know that no murderer has eternal life abiding in him.

DAY 1

WHY WE QUARREL AND FIGHT

There are two ways to get things in life: our way and God's way. If we are humble, our way dovetails with God's way. But if we are prideful, our way is opposed by God, since He opposes the proud.[139] Ask men and women on the street why they quarrel and fight with others and you will rarely hear anyone confess, "Because I don't get my way." But James said that's the reason.[140] It hurts our pride when we hear the word "No," whether spoken by a person or by God.

Hearing no from God seems unusual, but James suggested that our pride may spill over into our prayer life in the form of wrong motives. Our pride fools us into thinking we can ask God for something that is legitimate but that we plan to use for self-honoring ends. Therefore, the pride that creates conflicts with others also creates conflicts with God. Understandably, this is a delicate subject. What is the one-word answer that explains why we don't like to discuss, much less be accused of, pride?

P _ _ _ _

That's right: pride. Like a deceived man who doesn't know he is deceived, a prideful man has too much pride to repent of pride.

PRIDE AND RELATIONSHIPS

James ended the last part of his letter with a reference to peacemakers "whose fruit is righteousness" (James 3:18). But reports of something much different than peace were reaching James. There were apparently serious "quarrels and conflicts" (James 4:1) among the believers to whom he wrote. Through two rhetorical questions, what did James say is the source for the fighting that was occurring in the church?[141]

"Pleasures" is a fairly literal translation of the Greek word that indicates the source of their conflicts.[T53] We think of "pleasures" as things that make us feel good in a luxurious or expensive sense. That's really too narrow for what James had in mind. "Desires" or "preferences" would be more accurate, as in the formal language of decades ago: "What is your pleasure (desire, preference)?"

That which creates quarrels and conflicts among people (Christian or not) is insisting on our personal desires and reacting badly when we don't achieve them. This was the cause of the largest conflict the universe has ever known, as illustrated by Isaiah 14:12-15.[T54] There we read how the king of Babylon, who many believe to be a picture of Satan in conflict with God, exerted his will five times against God. In what five ways did the king exert his desires?[142]

- I will . . .

- I will . . .

- I will . . .

- I will . . .

- I will . . .

As illustrated by a prideful king and from your own experience, what does pride motivate us to do when we are in a relationship with others (see the first part of James 4:2)?[140]

At the heart of prideful desires is lust, or coveting.[T55] James used a strong word to describe the results of coveting and not getting: "murder."[140] In the following two passages of Scripture, what is murder used as a picture of?[T56]

- Matthew 5:21-22[143]

- 1 John 3:15[144]

LANGUAGE & LIT:[T53]

HEDONISM—The Greek word James used to describe the source of conflicts and quarrels (James 4:1,3) is *hedone*, from which comes our English word hedonism. The *American Heritage Dictionary* defines hedonism as "the pursuit of or devotion to pleasure, especially to the pleasures of the senses. The doctrine holding that behavior is motivated by the desire for pleasure and the avoidance of pain." In America we identify hedonism with the "eat, drink, and be merry" philosophy of life—doing whatever it takes to maximize pleasure and minimize pain. In the realm of relationships, hedonism is seen when we try to minimize the pain of unrealized expectations and unattained material things. Hedonism is the exact opposite of the biblical philosophy that says sometimes pain is for our good and should be seen as an ally, not an enemy (2 Corinthians 12:7-10).

STUDY TECHNIQUES:[T54]

TYPOLOGY—In biblical hermeneutics (the science of interpretation), a "type" is a prefiguring in the Old Testament of something made clear in the New Testament (the "antitype"). Types are most often related to prophetic events surrounding the life and ministry of Christ, such as Melchizedek (Genesis 14) being a type of Christ (Hebrews 7). But types can also foreshadow evil, such as the city of Babylon did in the Old Testament (see Revelation 17–18). In that same way, many Bible students believe that the king of Babylon, described in his arrogant pride against God in Isaiah 14:12-15, is a type of Satan. At the very least, the king of Babylon prefigures the "beast" who rules the Babylon of the last days (Revelation 13:4; 17:3). The king of Tyre is also considered by many to present a picture of the downfall of Satan (Ezekiel 28).

[145]**1 JOHN 2**

16 All that is in the world, the lust of the flesh and the lust of the eyes and the boastful pride of life, is not from the Father, but is from the world.

[146]**JAMES 4**

3 You ask and do not receive, because you ask with wrong motives, so that you may spend it on your pleasures.

[147]**LUKE 22**

42 "Father, if You are willing, remove this cup from Me; yet not My will, but Yours be done."

The apostle John summarized this scenario—see, want, fight to get—in a memorable way. How did he tie in self-centered pride with James' descriptions of earthly and heavenly wisdom?[131, 132, 133, 145]

We know that pride is at the root of conflicts and quarrels when we find ourselves saying, "I want . . ." and getting angry with anyone or anything that stands in our way.

PRIDE AND PRAYER

James *really* humbles us when he connects pride with prayer. How many of us ever stop to think that pride may be an issue in our praying (and lack of receiving)? Fill in the following based on James 4:2-3:[140, 146]

• We do not have because . . .

• We do not receive because . . .

What is the "wrong motive" that James identified?

Pride is pervasive. It can creep into how we view (use) other people for our own purposes ("I want what you have, or I want you to help me get what I want"). It also invades and taints our relationship with God ("I can't get what I want through my own efforts, so now I want You to help me get it").

The real question is this: Since few Christians would use words this blatant, what signs can we watch for that will help us detect when pride (personal desire and ambition) is making its subtle way into our walk with God and others?

BRINGING IT HOME

1. Though pride has many manifestations, in this lesson we are viewing it as the expression of self-will that uses God and others to accomplish self-centered desires. Those desires result in conflicts and quarrels with others and in unanswered prayer with God. What patterns of pride causing conflicts with others have you seen in your own life (think about extended family, your marriage and immediate family, the workplace, church, and other settings)?

What should you do when you discover that conflict has resulted from covetous desires on your part?

2. How would following the examples of Psalm 139:23-24[39] and Luke 22:42[147] help you to remove improper motives from your prayer life?

CROSS REFERENCES:[T55]

COVETING—The "lusting" that James described (James 4:2) is serious sin causing serious problems. "Lust" here translates the Greek verb *epithumeo*, which has *thumos* at its root: angry temper, fierce indignation, passion, rage. *Epithumeo* also shows up in the Septuagint, an early Greek translation of the Old Testament, where that translation renders the tenth commandment, "You shall not covet" (Exodus 20:17), as well as in Paul's reference to that commandment in Romans 7:7. It has often been noted by Bible students that when we break any one of the first nine commandments we also break the tenth. For what is idolatry, murder, theft, adultery—what is any sin?—if it is not first desiring something that is not ours, whether a person, a piece of property, an experience, a feeling, or a reputation? At that level, it is easy to see how breaking one of God's Ten Commandments could cause quarrels and conflicts.

LANGUAGE & LIT:[T56]

HYPERBOLE—James' use of "murder" (James 4:2) is an example of the figure of speech called hyperbole. Hyperbole is the use of exaggeration for emphasis or effect (for example, "I'm hungry enough to eat a horse!" or "I'm dead tired!" or "I'm going to shoot him when I find him!"). James' original readers weren't really killing one another, but they were pursuing their own desires with little regard to the harm it might do to one another emotionally and spiritually. James wanted to bring out the seriousness of their actions, and hyperbole offered a dramatic way to do it.

DAILY READING

Read Mark 7:20-23[49] and note the kind of company that pride (or arrogance) keeps.

DAY 2

WHAT GOD GIVES THE HUMBLE

[148]JEREMIAH 3; 31

3:20 "Surely, as a woman treacherously departs from her lover, so you have dealt treacherously with Me, O house of Israel," declares the LORD.

31:31-32 "Behold, days are coming," declares the LORD, "when I will make a new covenant with the house of Israel and the house of Judah, not like the covenant which I made with their fathers in the day I took them by the hand to bring them out of the land of Egypt, My covenant which they broke, although I was a husband to them," declares the LORD.

[149]JAMES 4

4 You adulteresses, do you not know that friendship with the world is hostility toward God? Therefore whoever wishes to be a friend of the world makes himself an enemy of God.

[150]REVELATION 3

15-16 "I know your deeds, that you are neither cold nor hot; I wish that you were cold or hot. So because you are lukewarm, and neither hot nor cold, I will spit you out of My mouth."

A key theme in James' letter is the contrast between God's way and the world's way of living (heavenly wisdom versus earthly "wisdom"). He made reference to remaining unstained by the world (1:27), referred to the world of iniquity (3:6), and called the "wisdom" of the world demonic (3:15). In 4:4-6, what is behind such firm and unequivocal language? These verses in James are at once some of the most important and most difficult to understand of his epistle. In order to make this lesson more profitable as we look at the details, here is a summary of how verses 4-6 fit into this portion of his letter:

- Verses 1-3: Your pride has become evident as you have lusted after what you do not have. God has even closed His ear to your prayers because of your prideful spirit.

- Verses 4-6: God has high standards for you. You are, in a sense, "married" to Him and He will not tolerate your affection for the world. In truth, He longs for a close relationship with you. But don't be discouraged by His high standards; He will give grace to you that is greater than His demands. But if you reject His grace, you will continue to experience His opposition (as you have already by His refusal to answer your prayers).

- Verses 7-10: Therefore, submit yourselves to God, and the Devil and his tactics will cease to characterize you. Repent of your prideful behavior and you will find the Lord meeting your every need.

GOD AND THE PROUD

God uses the most intimate language possible, in both the Old and the New Testaments, to picture His relationship with His people. How is God pictured in Jeremiah 3:20 and 31:31-32?[148]

As portrayed in Ephesians 5:22-33 (see appendix A), what is the relationship of Christ to the church?

No breach of the marriage covenant is so shocking to a husband as that of adultery, yet that is what God's people in the Old Testament had committed against their "husband," God. He had tenderly led Israel by the hand out of slavery in Egypt and had given her everything she needed, only to find that she had become a prostitute—a spiritual adulteress, a worshiper of other idols (2 Chronicles 21:11; Isaiah 1:21; Jeremiah 3:1; Ezekiel 16:28). An entire book of the Old Testament, Hosea, is devoted to illustrating Israel's adultery and God's faithfulness to her.

When James called Christians "adulteresses" (James 4:4), he was speaking out of the Old Testament context of believers as the "wife" of God. Instead of worshiping idols, what had the church given her affections to, according to James?[149]

What did James mean by "friendship with the world"?[149]

If you are friends with the world, you are the enemy of

_____.[T57]

If you are friends with God, you are the enemy of the

_____.

Is there room in this equation for compromise, for being friends with both?

If you are friends with both, you are also the

_____ of both.

What did Christ have to say to His bride in Laodicea about her desire to live "in the middle"—lukewarm, neither hot nor cold?[150]

One of the primary characteristics of God in the Old Testament is His faithfulness to Israel.[T58] James wanted Christians to know that God was still madly in love with His bride, His people, in spite of the sins they committed. What did Paul say about God's heart toward us even when we were His enemies?[94]

POINT OF INTEREST:[T57]

WHO'S RUNNING THE WORLD?—When we consider the truth of 1 John 5:19, it's not hard to understand why James said that becoming a friend of the world is to become an enemy of God. John the apostle said that "the whole world lies in the power of the evil one." "World" here is not the planet but the ordered, sin-based system that Satan has directed and empowered since the fall of Adam and Eve in the Garden of Eden. It is the world that God gave His only Son to save. It is the world that Satan tempted Jesus with while He fasted in the desert (Luke 4:1-13). It is a world with a value system totally at odds with the kingdom of God. So to embrace this world as a friend is to embrace the opposite of God, or to become the enemy of God. Many believers need to think carefully about the affection they feel toward the world system that is all around us. We are to be in the world but not of the world.

LANGUAGE & LIT:[T58]

GOD'S LOYAL LOVE—Many believers know what is perhaps the most important Greek word in the New Testament, *agape*, referring to unconditional love. But most are unfamiliar with its counterpart in the Old Testament, *hesed*, the loyal love, or loving-kindness, of God. *Hesed* is based on the covenant promises God made to Abraham, the father of the Jewish people and of all those who have faith in the one true God. It finds its ultimate expression in Jeremiah 31:36-37, where God tells Israel that as long as the heavens and earth exist He will be loyal in His love to them. For this reason, believers can know that God is One who pursues His beloved with desire and passion—because He is a loyal lover.

[151]**EXODUS 20; 34**

20:5 "You shall not worship [idols] or serve them; for I, the Lord your God, am a jealous God, visiting the iniquity of the fathers on the children, on the third and the fourth generations of those who hate Me."

34:14 "You shall not worship any other god, for the Lord, whose name is Jealous, is a jealous God."

[152]**JAMES 4**

6 [God] gives a greater grace. Therefore [the Scripture] says, "GOD IS OPPOSED TO THE PROUD, BUT GIVES GRACE TO THE HUMBLE."

[153]**PROVERBS 11**

2 When pride comes, then comes dishonor, but with the humble is wisdom.

[154]**PROVERBS 29**

23 A man's pride will bring him low, but a humble spirit will obtain honor.

[155]**ISAIAH 2**

17 The pride of man will be humbled and the loftiness of men will be abased; and the Lord alone will be exalted in that day.

The Old Testament teaches that God "jealously desires the Spirit[T59] which He has made to dwell in us." While this does not quote a specific Old Testament passage, how do Exodus 20:5 and 34:14[151] portray God's desire for the purity of His bride?

We don't normally think of jealousy as a positive attribute. How does God's jealousy differ from that of a person?

GOD AND THE HUMBLE

If God is eager to have a relationship with us, we can expect Him to meet our needs and care for us when we are tempted to turn to the world. What is the purpose of the grace that God promises to give?[152] How does His grace keep us from becoming adulterous?

God gives grace to the humble.[152] In the context of James' words in 4:1-5, how would you characterize the humble person, the one who can expect to receive grace from God?

What do the following verses contribute to your understanding of James' words?

• Proverbs 11:2[153]

• Proverbs 29:23[154]

• Isaiah 2:17[155]

BRINGING IT HOME

1. People are hesitant to discuss their own humility—it sounds like they are proud of it, thus negating what they profess to have! Those people are more likely possessors of false humility than of true humility, for true humility is a recognition and acceptance of one's rightful place before God. In what area(s) of life do you feel you have learned to be humble and have received God's grace to overcome temptations to worldly pride and behavior?

2. In what area(s) do you find yourself yielding to the temptation to be friends with the world?

   How does knowing that friends of the world are enemies of God affect your thinking about yielding to those temptations?

3. How is it possible for you to live in the world and enjoy what has been discovered, invented, and produced without becoming a "friend" of the world? Where is the line drawn, and how do you know when you have crossed it?

STUDY TECHNIQUES:[T59]

WHAT DOES GOD DESIRE?— Bible translations differ on their rendering of James 4:5. The *New American Standard Bible* (NASB) and the *New International Version* (NIV) have similar translations except for the word "Spirit/spirit." The NASB capitalizes it, while the NIV does not capitalize it. What's the difference? The NASB suggests that God has given the Holy Spirit to believers, and when they live in disobedience, the Father longs for renewed fellowship with believers through the Spirit whom He gave. The NIV's translation most likely refers to a spirit of love or devotion that is present between, say, husbands and wives but has been lost due to sin. God jealously desires for the devoted love to be restored. In either case, a correct rendering of the verse sees God as the pursuer of His people, jealously seeking to give grace to the humble.

DAILY READING

Read Proverbs 1:20-33 (see appendix A). Mark the instances of the foolish rejecting the attempts of wisdom to provide safety and refuge from the world.

[156]**PROVERBS 3**

34 Though [the LORD] scoffs at the scoffers, yet He gives grace to the afflicted.

[157]**2 CORINTHIANS 7**

11 Behold what earnestness this very thing, this godly sorrow, has produced in you: what vindication of yourselves, what indignation, what fear, what longing, what zeal, what avenging of wrong! In everything you demonstrated yourselves to be innocent in the matter.

[158]**ROMANS 7**

24 Wretched man that I am! Who will set me free from the body of this death?

DAY 3

TEN WAYS TO HUMBLE YOURSELF

If James is ever going to be accused of being a sourpuss and a party pooper, it will be in this section of his letter. But if we read his words and come away with that perception of him, it reveals more about us than it does about him. For James' stern words are totally consistent with Old and New Testament expressions concerning what people should do when they find themselves at odds with God. In a word, they should repent.

Repentance and humility are intimately connected. It takes humility to repent, and repentance is a sign of humility. James was continuing in his efforts to motivate his readers to live out what they said they believed. He had exposed their sin of worldliness and covetous greed and had revealed their posture as the enemies of God. He had even given them the book of Proverbs' take on pride and humility.[152, 156] Now it was time for them to show their humility, not just talk about it. Thus, he gave them ten ways to humble themselves.

REASONS FOR REPENTANCE

Someone once described a Puritan as a person who lives in mortal fear that someone, somewhere is enjoying life. This caricature is not based on truth but on the false perception of joy held by the world. This false perception is that joy is the enjoyment of selfish pleasures.

True joy is based in a deep-seated knowledge of the holy, and an understanding of holiness includes a realization of the gravity of sin. Only the person who understands the seriousness of sin, and has repented of sin before a holy God and been cleansed of its guilt and shame, can experience true joy. James was certainly acquainted with biblical joy (1:2; 5:13), and he longed for his readers to know it as well. But he knew that the road to the city of joy leads through the valley of repentance.

Repentance[T60] (changing one's mind about sin) and confession[T61] (agreeing with God about sin) can easily be mischaracterized as nothing more than mental transactions. But there is more to repentance than that—where the head goes, the body must follow. List all the ways that Paul observed repentance manifesting itself in the life of the believers in Corinth.[157]

When Paul wrote about his own struggle with sin in Romans 7, what did he call himself?[158] (Note: The adjective Paul used in Romans 7:24 is from the same family as the verb translated "Be miserable" in James 4:9.[T62] Thus, Paul agreed with James about the believer's response to sin.)

One of the clearest statements about the connections among sin, sorrow, and salvation is in Paul's second New Testament letter to the Corinthians:

> Though I caused you sorrow by my letter, I do not regret it; though I did regret it—for I see that that letter caused you sorrow, though only for a while—I now rejoice, not that you were made sorrowful, but that you were made sorrowful to the point of repentance; for you were made sorrowful according to the will of God, so that you might not suffer loss in anything through us. For the sorrow that is according to the will of God produces a repentance without regret, leading to salvation, but the sorrow of the world produces death.
> (2 Corinthians 7:8-10)

Follow Paul's reasoning (and note how it parallels James') by noting the following:

• What did Paul's earlier letter cause?

• Was the effect permanent or temporary?

• What was the ultimate result of his letter?

LANGUAGE & LIT:[T60]

REPENTANCE—Knowing the meaning of the Greek word for repentance—*metanoia*—is helpful in understanding the concept. It comes from *metanoeo*. The preposition *meta* ("against") and the verb *noeo* ("to perceive," "to think") combine to yield "to change one's mind." Great discussions have been had among theologians concerning the place of repentance in salvation. Repentance and faith should be seen as two sides of the same coin (Acts 20:21), for one cannot exercise faith without changing one's mind from what one previously believed. The behavioral changes accompanying and completing repentance are nothing more than the works of which James spoke.

LANGUAGE & LIT:[T61]

CONFESSION—The Greek word for confession explains its root meaning; *homologeo* consists of *homo* ("same") and *logeo* ("speak"). Therefore, confession is simply to speak the same thing as. In the case of Christian confession of sin, we say the same thing about our sin that God says. (In corporate, liturgical confession of our faith we say the same thing as the rest of the church says.) A classic example of confession occurred when the Lord sent the prophet Nathan to say what God thought about David's sin with Bathsheba (2 Samuel 12). After hearing God's view through Nathan, David said the same thing: "I have sinned against the LORD" (verse 13).

159 MATTHEW 27

24 When Pilate saw that he was accomplishing nothing, but rather that a riot was starting, he took water and washed his hands in front of the crowd, saying, "I am innocent of this Man's blood; see to that yourselves."

160 MATTHEW 5

4 "Blessed are those who mourn, for they shall be comforted."

161 MARK 14

72 Immediately a rooster crowed a second time. And Peter remembered how Jesus had made the remark to him, "Before a rooster crows twice, you will deny Me three times." And he began to weep.

162 PSALM 30

5 [The LORD's] anger is but for a moment, His favor is for a lifetime; weeping may last for the night, but a shout of joy comes in the morning.

163 PSALM 139

1-4 O LORD, You have searched me and known me. You know when I sit down and when I rise up; You understand my thought from afar. You scrutinize my path and my lying down, and are intimately acquainted with all my ways. Even before there is a word on my tongue, behold, O LORD, You know it all.

164 JOB 31; 34

31:4 Does [God] not see my ways and number all my steps?
34:21 His eyes are upon the ways of a man, and He sees all his steps.

• Did the Corinthians regret Paul's actions?

• What does repentance lead to?

RIGHT WAYS TO REPENT

While Old Testament wisdom authors were not unwilling to make lists (see Proverbs 6:16; 30:7,15,18,21,24,29), James wasn't following that pattern here. His ten ways to humble oneself are drawn from the ten imperative verbs[T63] he used to paint a picture of godly sorrow in the life of the believer. Let's identify all ten:

1. Submit. To whom?

2. Resist. Whom? With what effect? (Who had they been resisting?)

3. Draw near. To whom? What will happen then?

4. Cleanse your hands. What is this a picture of?[159]

5. Purify your hearts. Who needs to do this? What will they be if they don't do this?[32]

6. Be miserable. Recall Romans 7:24.[158]

7. Mourn. What will happen to those who mourn?[160]

8. Weep. What was Peter's response to his sin of denying Christ?[161]

9. Change laughter to mourning and joy to gloom. What comes on the morning after the mourning?[162]

10. Humble yourselves. Before whom? With what result?

While James' admonitions may seem strident to the ears of the modern church, remember that he wrote in a day when "sackcloth and ashes" was not a metaphor for repentance but a manual for repentance. James wrote like his kindred spirits, the Old Testament prophets, who called on Israel to repent visibly and seriously over sin. James would have the New Testament church repent no less genuinely.

BRINGING IT HOME

1. If you are a parent, you know the challenge of helping children learn the difference between being sorry for what they did wrong (godly sorrow) and being sorry they got caught (worldly sorrow). We must also learn this difference when we are born again and become babes in Christ. Where are you in that process? Which comes to mind first when you sin: sorrow for the sin or sorrow (anger, resentment, regret) that your sin has been discovered?

2. Another test in our understanding of humility that leads to repentance is the question of timing. When do you repent of sin—when you commit the sin or when the sin is found out? What would an understanding of Psalm 139:1-4[163] and Job 31:4 and 34:21[164] have on the imperative to repent when we have sinned?

LANGUAGE & LIT:[T62]

TWO MISERABLE WORDS— Paul used the adjective *talaiporos* ("wretched"), and James used the verb *talaiporeo* ("be miserable"). The connection between the two is clear. Because of Paul's sin, he saw the wretchedness of his condition as a sinner before God. James' readers failed to make that connection. Their pride and arrogance kept them from seeing themselves as they truly were. So he told them, in effect, "Be miserable! Prove that you understand the gravity of your sinful actions!"

LANGUAGE & LIT:[T63]

IMMEDIATE RESPONSE—Greek verbs have tenses just like English (past, present, future, and so on). One Greek tense not found in English is the *aorist* tense, which looks at actions as a unit, an event in time. It could be an event lasting a thousand years, so the length of time is not the issue. Most important is viewing it as a completed event. Linking the *aorist* tense with the imperative mood produces a "Do it now!" effect. All ten verbs James used are *aorist imperatives* meaning "Do them all—*now!*"

DAILY READING

Read 1 Corinthians 5 (see appendix A). Note the parallels between Paul's instructions to the Corinthian church and James' instructions to the dispersed Jewish Christians.

DAY 4

HOW TO KNOW YOU ARE NOT HUMBLE

[165] **JAMES 4**

11 Do not speak against one another, brethren. He who speaks against a brother or judges his brother, speaks against the law and judges the law; but if you judge the law, you are not a doer of the law but a judge of it.

[166] **MATTHEW 18**

15-17 "If your brother sins, go and show him his fault in private; if he listens to you, you have won your brother. But if he does not listen to you, take one or two more with you, SO THAT BY THE MOUTH OF TWO OR THREE WITNESSES EVERY FACT MAY BE CONFIRMED. If he refuses to listen to them, tell it to the church; and if he refuses to listen even to the church, let him be to you as a Gentile and a tax collector."

[167] **GALATIANS 6**

1 Brethren, even if anyone is caught in any trespass, you who are spiritual, restore such a one in a spirit of gentleness; each one looking to yourself, so that you too will not be tempted.

[168] **PROVERBS 17**

27 He who restrains his words has knowledge, And he who has a cool spirit is a man of understanding.

[169] **PROVERBS 10**

19 Where there are many words, transgression is unavoidable, But he who restrains his lips is wise.

We have an uncanny knack for identifying sin in others before seeing the same sin in ourselves. If we're driving ten miles per hour over the speed limit, we shake our heads at the guy who passes us. If the pastor preaches a sermon on commitment, we who attend only the Sunday worship service nod our head in agreement, wondering, *Where are the truly committed?* Why are we such experts on the sins of others and not on our own?

The roots of our disease are in our fleshly dispositions, of course. We justify, rationalize, excuse, and otherwise avoid the painful process of self-correction (who has time to correct himself when so many others need attention?). Apparently James' readers were inclined to do the same. In order to keep them from turning their attention to the speck of pride in their brother's or sister's eye, he encouraged them (and us) to focus first on the logjam in their own.

LAWBREAKERS AND FALSE JUDGES

James must have gotten word that members of churches were speaking ill of each other. There are two problems with that sort of behavior:[165] First, when we speak ill of another person, we break God's Law ourselves. And second, by breaking the Law, we set ourselves up as judges of the Law's worth. Both actions indicate that we are too proud to place ourselves under the scrutiny of God's standards.

What, specifically, were James' original readers doing? "Slander," used by some translations, is only part of the story. The *New American Standard Bible*'s "Do not speak against one another" is more accurate and inclusive of the possibilities. Slander is speaking falsely about a person in a way that damages his or her reputation. Speaking ill of another is broader; it can include saying things that are true but doing it in a harsh or detrimental way and for wrong motives.[T64]

Under the guise of "sharing" or "asking for prayer," how do Christians sometimes spread information negatively about fellow believers?[T65]

The law that James said we violate and judge is the law he mentioned in 2:8.[61] Explain how speaking against another person violates that law.

Explain how violating the "royal law" of love establishes us as a judge over that law. (Hint: If I violate a law, I have made a judgment about the necessity or appropriateness of the law's content.)[T66]

What hypocritical reaction do we have if someone violates that law at *our* expense?

Provision is made in Scripture for us to help one another with moral and spiritual progress. According to Matthew 18:15-17,[166] what should you do if you know someone is involved in willful sin?

Step 1:

Step 2:

Step 3:

With what sort of attitude should we approach someone who is living in error (Galatians 1:6)?[167]

Christians sometimes act on the mistaken notion that because something is true it deserves to be repeated. What do these verses suggest about that idea?

• Proverbs 17:27[168]

• Proverbs 10:19[169]

CROSS REFERENCES:[T64]
SPEECH—For additional insights on speech, see the following verses: Exodus 20:16; 1 Kings 21:8-15; Psalm 10:7; 12; 15:3; 50:19-20; 57:4; 59:7; 64:3-4; 140:11; Proverbs 6:16,19; Ephesians 4:31; 1 Timothy 3:11; 2 Timothy 3:3; 1 Peter 2:1.

POINT OF INTEREST:[T65]
SLOW TO SPEAK—James' words in 1:19 ("everyone must be quick to hear, slow to speak") bear particular relevance to his discussion here concerning speaking ill of others. This, of course, applies to slanderous or otherwise hurtful information. The more subtle arena, however, is in sharing or speaking of something that is true. If it is true that "all truth is God's truth" (and it is), then when we know something about a person that is true, we become a steward of something that God has an interest in. As servants, then, our responsibility is to ask Him, "Lord, why have You delivered this truth to me? What should I do with it now that I know it? Make me a good steward." God Himself does not tell everything He knows (Deuteronomy 29:29; Job 26:14), and it is the hallmark of wise people when they know how to conceal a matter (Proverbs 25:9). We must avoid the temptation of "celebrity" status by being the one "in the know" with all the latest information. Our gossip-driven age tempts us to participate in what has no place in the kingdom of God.

[170]**PROVERBS 26**

20 For lack of wood the fire goes out, and where there is no whisperer, contention quiets down.

[171]**LUKE 6**

39-42 [Jesus] also spoke a parable to them: "A blind man cannot guide a blind man, can he? Will they not both fall into a pit? A pupil is not above his teacher; but everyone, after he has been fully trained, will be like his teacher. Why do you look at the speck that is in your brother's eye, but do not notice the log that is in your own eye? Or how can you say to your brother, 'Brother, let me take out the speck that is in your eye,' when you yourself do not see the log that is in your own eye? You hypocrite, first take the log out of your own eye, and then you will see clearly to take out the speck that is in your brother's eye."

LAWGIVER AND TRUE JUDGE

The ultimate problem with our judging God's standards is that they are His, not ours! There is no display of pride more serious than when a human being puts himself or herself in the place of God. Remember the sin of the king of Babylon (who typifies Satan) discussed earlier? What was the last of his five "I wills"?[142]

James drew on his knowledge of Isaiah to confirm a foundational belief for his Jewish-Christian readers. List and connect with lines the key terms in Isaiah 33:22 and James 4:12:

If God is the sole lawgiver and judge, James' readers' actions deserved his final question of rebuke (here taken from Eugene Peterson's *The Message*): "God is in charge of deciding human destiny. Who do you think you are to meddle in the destiny of others?" Who, indeed! It is painfully presumptuous of us to establish our own standards and then judge others by those standards, especially since we are bereft of any power to save or destroy in light of our "judgments." We have no power to reward or condemn anyone.

BRINGING IT HOME

1. Sometimes our judgments of others are made inwardly and remain there, fermenting and building up pressure likely to be released at an inopportune time. Is that true for you? If so, using Scripture's admonition to speak the truth in love (Ephesians 4:15), perhaps you should consider a heart-to-heart conversation with a person you find yourself continually judging. (WARNING: Conversations like this are not a license to criticize or condemn! They are an opportunity to take the initiative in seeking common ground and to serve, with the goal of strengthening the relationship.)

2. Have you spoken inappropriately about another person (something untrue, something exaggerated, something that's true but should have been kept private)? James' words suggest that all such speaking is sin. Go as soon as possible and make amends where damage through ill-spoken words has occurred. Likewise, determine not to be on the receiving end of such words. Remember Proverbs 26:20.[170]

POINT OF INTEREST:[T66]

GOLDEN RULE—The Golden Rule—"Treat others the same way you want them to treat you," Luke 6:31—repeats the premise of Leviticus 19:18. No one wants to be slandered or have information about his or her life broadcast to others. Therefore, no one should do that to another.

DAILY READING

Read Luke 6:39-42.[171] Mark the truths that support James' points discussed in this lesson.

HOW TO HOPE WITH HUMILITY

[172]**JAMES 4**

14 You do not know what your life will be like tomorrow. You are just a vapor that appears for a little while and then vanishes away.

[173]**PSALM 90**

10-12 As for the days of our life, they contain seventy years, or if due to strength, eighty years, yet their pride is but labor and sorrow; for soon it is gone and we fly away. Who understands the power of Your anger and Your fury, according to the fear that is due You? So teach us to number our days, that we may present to You a heart of wisdom.

[174]**ISAIAH 40**

6-7 A voice says, "Call out." Then he answered, "What shall I call out?" All flesh is grass, and all its loveliness is like the flower of the field. The grass withers, the flower fades, when the breath of the LORD blows upon it; surely the people are grass.

[175]**JAMES 4**

15 You ought to say, "If the Lord wills, we will live and also do this or that."

[176]**ACTS 18**

21 Taking leave of [the Jews of Ephesus] and saying, "I will return to you again if God wills," [Paul] set sail from Ephesus.

Regardless of what time of the day or night you are reading these words, on one of your mind's back burners are thoughts about the future. Your thoughts range from what you'll do in a few minutes to what you'll do in a few years. We never stop thinking about the future, and in spite of the efforts of time-management seminars, we learn that time cannot be managed—we can only manage what we do with time.

James' final words in chapter 3 of his letter concern human pride and our hopes for the future. Not only is it necessary to submit to God and to fellow believers with humility in the realm of the present—that which we can see today—but it is even more necessary to submit to that which we cannot see and therefore cannot predict, dictate, or control, namely, the future.

PRESUMING WITH PRIDE

James was not about to say that it is wrong to make plans for the future. As a student of the Old Testament, he was well aware of the verses in Proverbs that encourage planning (see Proverbs 16:1-4,9). But in almost every proverb that addresses planning for the future, you find the one element that is missing from the planning process described by James. Compare the following verses and, under each one, note the positive or negative aspects of each:

Proverbs 16:3	James 4:13
Commit your works to the Lord, and your plans will be established.	Come now, you who say, "Today or tomorrow we will go to such and such a city, and spend a year there and engage in business and make a profit."

There might have been businesspeople in the churches James was writing to—those for whom planning was critical to success.[T67] In the text of James 4:13, circle as many elements of business planning as you can find. How thorough do they appear to be?

What is the one critical element that, as Christians, James' readers had left out?

Whether for business, family, vocation, education, pleasure—for whatever reason we plan for the future—why is it presumptuous on our part to say, "I will . . ."?

RECONCILING WITH REALITY

The reality is that we do not know whether we will or will not accomplish what we plan, because only God knows and directs the future.

To what did James compare human life?[172]

Think about a mist or fog. What was James trying to say when he compared us to a mist?

What do Psalm 90:10-12[173] and Isaiah 40:6-7[174] add to your understanding of the brevity and frailty of human life?

Despite the brevity and frailty of life, we are not adrift in the universe, subject to the arbitrary results of accidents and other events. What verses in the Bible give you confidence of God's overarching sovereignty and control of the affairs of your life?

HISTORY & CULTURE:[T67]

BIBLICAL BUSINESS—In our day of advanced communication and commerce, we somehow think that we invented business. But life has always included commerce in some form or another, and the biblical era is no exception. From the days of the Midianite traders who on their way to Egypt bought Joseph from his brothers (Genesis 37:28), to the days of the merchants who turned the Jerusalem temple into a "robbers den" (Mark 11:17), businessmen and businesswomen have been making and executing plans for profit. Other New Testament examples of believers in business include Aquila and Priscilla (Acts 18:2,18; Romans 16:3) and Lydia (Acts 16:14). The apostle Paul himself was a businessman, a maker of tents, who plied his trade to support himself in his ministry (Acts 18:1-4).

LANGUAGE & LIT:[T68]

BOASTING IN ARROGANCE— The *New American Standard Bible*'s translation of James 4:16 ("boast in your arrogance") is different from that of some other translations and gives us significant clues about James' meaning. It is important to note the ground (reason) of the boasting done by James' readers. More than fifteen times in the New Testament the verb "boast," preceded or followed by the preposition "in," signifies the reason for the boast (for example, 1 Corinthians 1:31, "boast in the Lord"; 2 Corinthians 12:9, "boast about my weaknesses"). In this case, James said the believers were boasting in (or about) their arrogance. Their first mistake was to leave God out of their plans; their second was to boast about it!

[177]**1 CORINTHIANS 4**
19 I will come to you soon, if the Lord wills, and I shall find out, not the words of those who are arrogant but their power.

[178]**ACTS 19**
21 Paul purposed in the spirit to go to Jerusalem after he had passed through Macedonia and Achaia, saying, "After I have been there, I must also see Rome."

[179]**ROMANS 15**
28 When I have finished this, and have put my seal on this fruit of theirs, I will go on by way of you to Spain.

[180]**1 CORINTHIANS 16**
5,8 I will come to you after I go through Macedonia, for I am going through Macedonia. . . . But I will remain in Ephesus until Pentecost.

[181]**ROMANS 1**
9-10 Unceasingly I make mention of you, always in my prayers making request, if perhaps now at last by the will of God I may succeed in coming to you.

[182]**ROMANS 15**
30,32 Strive together with me in your prayers to God for me, . . . so that I may come to you in joy by the will of God and find refreshing rest in your company.

[183]**JAMES 4**
16-17 You boast in your arrogance; all such boasting is evil. Therefore, to one who knows the right thing to do and does not do it, to him it is sin.

HOPING WITH HUMILITY

If it is arrogant and prideful on our part to predict the future without including God in our plans, what reflects true humility as we look at the next hours, days, or years? The apostle Paul was a model of what James suggested in verse 15.[175] What evidence of humility do you see in the way he made plans in Acts 18:21[176] and 1 Corinthians 4:19[177]?

But consider also Acts 19:21,[178] Romans 15:28,[179] and 1 Corinthians 16:5,8.[180] What is missing from these verses that was found in the previous ones?

However, in the case of Acts 19:21, what light does Romans 1:9-10[181] shed?

And concerning Romans 15:28, what insight on Paul can you find in Romans 15:30,32?[182]

Regardless of Paul's exact words in any given situation, what can you conclude about Paul's perspective on planning as a Christian?

How did James' own half brother, Jesus, model "hope with humility"?[147]

POSTSCRIPT ON PRESUMPTION

It is certainly one thing (and bad enough) to boast. It is another thing (and worse) to boast "in your arrogance" (James 4:16).[183, T68] Because the kind of boasting James wrote about is presumption based on the exclusion of God from life, it is evil.[T69] A final rebuke is issued by James: "You've been warned. If you know it's wrong to live pridefully, yet continue to do it, you are living in sin." While his direct application was probably to the issue of planning he had just addressed, his final word is consistent with the entire chapter dealing with pride.

BRINGING IT HOME

1. List some of the plans you are considering for the following periods of time:

   • Later today:

   • Next week:

   • Next year:

   • Five years from now:

   What efforts are you making to include God in the planning process?

2. The shorter the range of our plans, the less likely we are to consciously take steps to include God in the process. For instance, you probably don't pray about each item to select in the grocery store today, yet you probably will pray often about the process of selling your home and moving to a new city next year. What makes the difference? How can the believer maintain an attitude of dependency upon God to remain dependent on His guidance and provision even in the smallest areas of life?

3. Given the last exhortation in this chapter (verse 17),[183] are there areas of your life (regarding planning or otherwise) in which you know what to do but are not doing it? What do you believe Scripture is calling you to do about those areas?

HISTORY & CULTURE:[T69]

LEAVING GOD OUT OF LIFE— Humanism as a school of thought arose during the Renaissance (fourteenth–sixteenth centuries) as a result of a renewed interest in the study of the literature, art, and civilization of ancient Greece and Rome. It received a boost in the period of the Enlightenment (eighteenth century), when science and reason began to take precedence over matters of faith. Humanism is characterized by a dependence on human ability to achieve human goals. Many believe that America has been, culturally speaking, in a humanistic, or post-Christian period, for the last several decades—a time when God is increasingly left out of the thinking of many and when major national concerns are undertaken in human strength and wisdom alone. James had words of warning to all humanists (James 4:6) and an invitation to those of His people for whom humanism has become an influence (2 Chronicles 7:14).

DAILY READING

Read Matthew 6:25-34 (see appendix A). Meditate on how this passage speaks to the issue of priorities in the future and staying focused on God.

To the leader: You'll need sheets of paper, a flipchart or marker board, and markers.

1. James traced the source of quarreling among his readers to their selfish desires. The irony is that they could have had what they really needed if they had only asked God for it in a righteous way.
   - Choose a completion of the following sentence: In the list of my current spiritual struggles, pride is (a) at or near the top, (b) at or near the bottom, (c) somewhere in the middle.
   - Think of one conflict that you were involved in sometime in the past. What inner desire (or desires) motivated your part in the conflict?
   - First, on a sheet of paper, write a brief fictional prayer in which you ask for something that's legitimate but you ask for it with the wrong motives. Next, pass your sheet to the person on your right (everybody gets somebody else's prayer). Rewrite the prayer you have been handed in a way you think would be more acceptable to God. Last, take turns reading aloud the two versions of the prayers.

2. James accused his readers of spiritual adultery by worldliness. But God still loved them and wanted to give grace to them if they would humble themselves.
   - What does it mean for a person today to be a "friend of the world"? Why is this incompatible with being God's friend?
   - What is the connection between pride and worldliness?

3. In light of the grace available, James urged his readers to humble themselves, repent, and return to God.
   - According to the law of physics, a body will continue moving in the same direction unless a force acts against it. What kinds of forces does it take to make you do the turnaround of repentance when you have been sinning?
   - On a flipchart or marker board, list all ten of the imperative phrases in James 4:7-10 (1. Submit to God. 2. Flee from the Devil. And so forth.). For each one, come up with either a biblical story or an example out of your own life to illustrate the action.

4. James warned his readers against judging one another. That was simply not their responsibility, he said.
   - Why do human beings make bad judges?
   - Are there ever times when it's OK to say something negative about a fellow Christian? If so, when? And how is this different from the kind of judging James was talking about?

5. James also warned those who would plan for their future well-being in a presumptuous way. Given our human frailty, it's only reasonable to have a large measure of humility about how the future might turn out for us.
   - If you had to sum up your attitude toward the future in one word, what would it be? Even if you are more or less fearful about the future, do you take some things for granted (such as having good health or being able to earn a living)?
   - How can things like insurance, tenure, 401(k) plans, Social Security, and investment portfolios give us a false sense of security?
   - How can we integrate our faith into our planning for the future? In other ways, how can we be humble yet hopeful?

Close with three to five minutes of silent prayer in which group members are free to confess selfish desires, judgmentalism, presumption, or other manifestations of pride.

Wrap up with a brief spoken prayer of thanks to God for His willingness to forgive us and receive us back when we've done wrong.

INTRODUCTION TO UNIT 5
WISDOM IN PROSPERITY, PATIENCE, AND PRAYER
(JAMES 5)

Destination: To discover the natural rhythm of the spiritual life outlined by James: persecution, perseverance, and prayer.

It is time to step back from the letter of James and recall the point from which he started. Like a brilliant composer, James made the last chapter of his letter reprise his first. In chapter 1 of James there is tension—like a symphony beginning in a minor key. The church is not at home, dwelling in peace and security; it is scattered, driven from its homeland (Israel and Jerusalem) by persecution following the resurrection of Christ. And in its new home, the church is an alien presence, persecuted by the powerful residents of the area. In the face of persecution, James said, the church had to persevere, knowing that its testing had maturity as its goal.

But how to persevere? When people who have been floating with the current are suddenly forced to swim upstream, they discover that they lack the skills. Staying afloat in the current of Judaism is quite different than battling upstream as a Christian believer. (The casual movements required to tread water are nothing compared to the stroke and kick of the freestyle long-distance swimmer.) So James said to pray—ask God for the skill (the wisdom) to know how to persevere in the face of persecution. After all, the Christian life is a marathon, not a sprint. Persecution, perseverance, and prayer. This is the rhythm of the spiritual life that must be learned by all who would follow Jesus as Lord. "Remember," Jesus said, "'A slave is not greater than his master.' If they persecuted Me, they will also persecute you" (John 15:20).

But that was just James' introduction. The rest of his letter is spent explaining to his readers what not persevering looks like: favoritism, faith that does nothing, a tongue that could set a church on fire, and life skills learned from the Devil himself. Fighting, quarreling, boasting—was this a church or an exercise in living without God? If the latter, James thought they were doing a good job. But that's not what it was, and James knew it. He was writing to the babylike body of Christ, to believers being baptized by fire into the kingdom of God. "We do things differently in the kingdom, my brothers," James was in effect saying. And the curriculum is the same: persecution, perseverance, and prayer.

In chapter 5 we see the reprise. Look how eighteen of James' final verses parallel eight of his first:

	Chapter 1	Chapter 5
Persecution	1:2	5:1-6
Perseverance	1:3-4	5:7-12
Prayer	1:5-8	5:13-18

In chapter 1 we got hints of the themes to come; in chapter 5 we get the themes expanded. It's obvious, by virtue of James' beginning and ending with the same themes, what his central message to the church is: We are not called by Christ to anything less strenuous than what He was called to by His Father. And just as He proved His faith in the things He suffered (Hebrews 5:8), so must we. Faith not proven is faith not possessed.

Be patient, brethren, until the coming of the Lord. The farmer waits for the precious produce of the soil, being patient about it, until it gets the early and late rains. You too be patient; strengthen your hearts, for the coming of the Lord is near.

JAMES 5:7-8

DAY 1

LIFESTYLES OF THE RICH AND FOOLISH

184 JAMES 5

1 Come now, you rich, weep and howl for your miseries which are coming upon you.

185 JAMES 5

2-6 Your riches have rotted and your garments have become moth-eaten. Your gold and your silver have rusted; and their rust will be a witness against you and will consume your flesh like fire. It is in the last days that you have stored up your treasure! Behold, the pay of the laborers who mowed your fields, and which has been withheld by you, cries out against you; and the outcry of those who did the harvesting has reached the ears of the Lord of Sabaoth. You have lived luxuriously on the earth and led a life of wanton pleasure; you have fattened your hearts in a day of slaughter. You have condemned and put to death the righteous man; he does not resist you.

186 PROVERBS 3

27-28 Do not withhold good from those to whom it is due, when it is in your power to do it. Do not say to your neighbor, "Go, and come back, and tomorrow I will give it," when you have it with you.

There is ample evidence in James' letter that the believers to whom he wrote were being mistreated, even persecuted. And the rich of the regions where they lived appear to have been culpable. James clearly said in 2:6-7 that wicked, wealthy people were guilty of slandering God's name, even of hauling believers into court on (presumably) trumped-up charges. And this in spite of the fact that the church was catering to them on Sundays (2:2-5). Persecution by nonbelieving, wealthy people must have played a significant role in the overall difficult situation to which James referred in the opening verses of the letter (1:2-3).

James' judgment (in agreement with Peter; compare 1 Peter 4:17) began first with the household of God as he chastised the church for catering to the rich while discriminating against their own poor members (2:1-6). But now James had a word for the wicked wealthy ones who had been abusing his spiritual flock. In this section of his letter James took off his pastor's hat and donned the mantle of a prophet, showing the same fiery zeal that his half brother did when He cleansed the Jerusalem temple (Matthew 21:12-13).

WARNING TO THE WICKED WEALTHY

The identity of the people James was addressing needs to be established. What did he call his readers in 1:2,16,19; 2:1,5,14; 3:1,10,12; 4:11; 5:7,9-10,12 (see appendix A) that he does not call the wealthy in 5:1?[184]

What do you gather about the identity of the wealthy from the fact that James did not challenge them (in 5:1-6) to change, only recited their sins?

What are the "miseries"[184] that were coming upon them (see Revelation 20:11-15 in appendix A)?

It seems appropriate to conclude that the people James was writing to were not Christian believers.[T70] While Scripture addresses wealthy Christians in other places (for example, 1 Timothy 6:17-19), here James was issuing a warning to nonbelievers who used their positions of wealth to abuse the poor among them.

WAYS OF THE WICKED WEALTHY

The wealthy people James was addressing were guilty of four kinds of abuses:

1. The wealthy were hoarding their wealth (James 5:2-3).[185] Economically, life in biblical days was much different than it is today. In general terms, the average person was considered "poor"—the rich were the exception. What separated the two were resources at hand. If, at the beginning of the day, you faced the task of finding resources to make it through that day (food and so on), you were pretty much average (that is, poor). If, on the other hand, you had resources on hand to take you several or many days into the future, you were considered rich.[T71]

Rotting food, moth-eaten or mildewed clothing, and rusted metal are all signs of what?[185]

How could excess resources be used to benefit others?

In terms of faith in a God who knows the future, what is hoarding an evidence of?

2. The wealthy were withholding their wealth (James 5:4). For those with a Jewish background, like James and his readers, the prompt payment of laborers was a given. It would appear that some Christians had found work in the fields of wealthy landowners but were not being paid for the work they had done. For poor people who earned their food on a daily basis, prompt payment was a necessity.

What does Proverbs 3:27-28[186] teach about postponing the payment of anything that is owed to another?

CROSS REFERENCES:[T70]

PAGANS IN TROUBLE—God was not hesitant, through His Old Testament prophets, to address the spiritual condition and behavior (and resulting judgment) of pagan nations with whom His chosen people interacted. Therefore, James was being entirely consistent at this point in addressing the behavior of non-Christians in a letter addressed to the church, especially given his proclivity for Old Testament thinking.

For further study:
Isaiah 13–23; Jeremiah 46–51; Ezekiel 25–32; Amos 1:3–2:16; Obadiah 1–14; Nahum 3:1-10; Zephaniah 2:4-15

HISTORY & CULTURE:[T71]

GOLD, SILVER, AND CLOTHES—While clothes today are used as a sign of wealth, in biblical days they *were* wealth. That is, cloth and fabric were often viewed on the same plane as gold and silver (see 2 Kings 5:5,22; Acts 20:33). They were commodities used as currency. The hoarding of clothes as a form of wealth was repudiated by Jesus because of the waste that occurred when moths destroyed them (Matthew 6:19).

POINT OF INTEREST:[T72]

HOW MUCH DEBT?—Debate about debt in light of Romans 13:8 is plentiful. Many Christians believe that debt is acceptable if it is for an appreciating asset (for example, a house) that could be liquidated for more than the balance owed. Also, many do not count as debt monies that are owed but paid on time (for example, credit card debt). Others point to Proverbs 22:7 ("the borrower becomes the lender's slave"), saying that to the degree we owe anyone anything, we are not free. They say we should strive to be as free as possible from any encumbrance (including debt) that would hinder us from following the commands of the Master as His servants (Hebrews 12:1).

[187] **MATTHEW 5; ROMANS 12**
Matthew 5:39 "I say to you, do not resist an evil person; but whoever slaps you on your right cheek, turn the other to him also."

Romans 12:19 Never take your own revenge, beloved, but leave room for the wrath of God, for it is written, "VENGEANCE IS MINE, I WILL REPAY," says the Lord.

[188] **1 TIMOTHY 6**
9-10 Those who want to get rich fall into temptation and a snare and many foolish and harmful desires which plunge men into ruin and destruction. For the love of money is a root of all sorts of evil, and some by longing for it have wandered away from the faith and pierced themselves with many griefs.

What is the one debt that Christians are allowed to keep outstanding (Romans 13:8)?[64, T72]

3. The wealthy were wasting their wealth (James 5:5). While others were just managing to scrape by (if that), the wealthy were indulging themselves in luxury.

Perhaps this is the most subtle abuse of them all, and it's one we should especially consider. It is easy for us to look around and criticize indulgence in our society. But how about in our own lives? What guidelines do you use to balance the use of your own "wealth" on yourself versus helping to meet the needs of others?[T73]

4. The wealthy were mistreating others with their wealth (James 5:6). This is the worst of the four abuses because it involves deliberate malice against the innocent. Apparently the wealthy were using their influence in the legal system to take away what little the poor had so as to add to their own already ample stock. Yet the Christians were unwilling to seek revenge for mistreatment.

The use of economic leverage against those whom you know live by a nonretaliatory ethic is a double sin. How are Christians counseled to respond to harm brought against them by another (Matthew 5:39; Romans 12:19)?[187]

BRINGING IT HOME

1. James' discussion of (apparently) non-Christian, wealthy individuals who lived their lives self-centeredly would be easy to read for purely historical interest—as if it had little application to the believer today. But one thing makes his words relevant to the Christian: We have the same capacity to sin that non-Christians do. Just because believers have been born again into a faith relationship with Christ does not mean we are free from the temptations to self-centeredness, specifically material greed and abuse. Hopefully, the presence of the Holy Spirit, and a new set of kingdom values, will bring about significant changes—but self-control and generosity are disciplines and traits that must be learned and developed.

What do the words of 1 Timothy 6:9-10[188] (written to Timothy, a Christian church planter and pastor, by the apostle Paul) suggest to you about the danger that money represents to the believer?

2. What practical steps do you take to manage your own material assets in ways that reflect your values as a Christian?

3. Take a moment and whisper a prayer to the Lord: "Is there any debt outstanding that I should give immediate attention to? Have I failed in any way to distribute what You have entrusted to me in a manner that would most please You?" Then listen.

CROSS REFERENCES:[T73]

CONTENTMENT—Paul spoke of being content with what he had (Philippians 4:11-13), specifically mentioning food and clothing as the basics with which he could carry on in life (1 Timothy 6:8). How does Paul's level of contentment (food and clothing) translate into modern terms? What would be the equivalent for the contemporary Christian? Should there be an equivalent, or is the point of contentment a personal matter for each believer to decide upon individually? Our materially focused world forces us to reckon with this issue.

DAILY READING

Read Luke 16:19-31 (see appendix A). Mark those verses that underscore James' message in this part of his letter.

DAY 2

HOW TO WAIT LIKE A FARMER

The first paragraph of James 5 is a solemn warning to those who have hoarded, withheld, wasted, and used their wealth to mistreat others (James 5:1-6). In the next five verses, however, James offered a word of consolation and encouragement to believers who had been oppressed by such people. He used farmers, prophets, and Job as an example of patient perseverance—how to wait under adverse circumstances for something.

While few of us have been tyrannized and exploited like first-century Christians, we know what it is to be misunderstood, cheated, or deceived. How do you feel when you are the victim of injustice? Are you tempted to lash back—to get even by seeking revenge? James told us how to respond when we are mistreated. In this lesson we look at the example of farmers; in the next lesson, at Job and the prophets.

HOW TO BE PATIENT

James, in verse 7, gave us additional clues to understanding the preceding verses (5:1-6), which we looked at in our last lesson. What does "Therefore be patient . . ." (verse 7)[189] imply about James' readers' relationship to the abuses detailed in verses 1-6?

What does the use of the word "brethren" (verse 7)[189] imply about the spirituality of those described in verses 1-6?

It seems clear that James' readers were undergoing significant suffering and persecution of various sorts at the hands of powerful non-Christians in their vicinity. They were perhaps ruled over by them, employed by them, or persecuted by them in a religious sense. James wanted them to patiently persevere in their suffering.

In biblical lands the growing season for farmers lasted from early fall, when seed was sown, until the harvest the following year. Two periods of rain nurtured the crops: early rains in October and November, and late rains in April and May as the crop was maturing.[T74] What could the

---

farmer do between planting and harvest to "speed up" the production of his crops?

Just as a farmer must be patient in order to reap his harvest, so the Christian must be patient in the face of undeserved suffering. What is the event for which Christians patiently wait as a farmer waits for his harvest (verse 7)?[189]

WHY BE PATIENT

Tell a child to be patient and wait, and he or she will quickly learn to ask, "How long?" The very notion of patience suggests a situation out of the ordinary, a situation that is testing our patience. Therefore, we naturally want to know when the test will be over. James obviously understood this because he immediately supplied the answer, which becomes the reason why his readers were to be patient: Christians must be patient until the return of Jesus Christ.

List all the insights you find in 2 Thessalonians 1:5-10[190] that help explain why the Lord's return is a worthy focal point for those who suffer.

James said the Lord's return is "near" (James 5:8),[189,T75] but it has been nearly two thousand years since James wrote this. In light of 2 Peter 3:8-9,[191] what do those two thousand years equal on God's timetable?

Also, what reason did Peter give for why God might be exercising patience of His own with those who were persecuting James' readers?[191]

The next time you find yourself unjustly persecuted for any reason, what could you remember about God's desire

HISTORY & CULTURE:[T74]

EARLY AND LATTER RAINS—The rains in Israel came to have figurative as well as literal significance. The early (fall) rains and late (spring) rains ("early" and "late" refer to time relative to the planting/harvest cycle) were bookends on either side of the harsh Israelite summer. Almost no rain was expected from May through September in Israel, so the early rains relieved the summer drought and the spring rains filled the cisterns in anticipation of the approaching summer. The giving of the rains was a sign of God's blessing (Deuteronomy 28:12; Joel 2:23; Zechariah 10:1), as their withholding was a sign of His judgment (Deuteronomy 28:23-24; 1 Kings 17:1-16). The patience and righteousness of the farmer were both tested as he looked for the spring rains to complete the growth cycle of his crops.

POINT OF INTEREST:[T75]

HOW CLOSE IS "NEAR"?—The doctrine of imminency states that the next great event on God's timetable of history is the return of Christ (Romans 13:12; Hebrews 10:25; 1 Peter 4:7). Were the apostles mistaken in thinking that the return of Christ was to occur in their lifetime (for example, see 1 Thessalonians 4:15)? They would not have been wrong if they had thought that, nor would we. The "last days" (5:3) began with the first coming of Christ, and we have been in the "last days" ever since (Acts 1:11; Hebrews 1:2). That fact that nearly two thousand years have passed does not change the fact His return is imminent. And the fact that it is imminent should cause us to heed James' words all the more carefully (James 5:8-9).

[192] **1 THESSALONIANS 3**
13 . . . so that He may establish your hearts without blame in holiness before our God and Father at the coming of our Lord Jesus with all His saints.

[193] **ROMANS 12**
18 If possible, so far as it depends on you, be at peace with all men.

[194] **1 PETER 2**
20-23 What credit is there if, when you sin and are harshly treated, you endure it with patience? But if when you do what is right and suffer for it you patiently endure it, this finds favor with God. For you have been called for this purpose, since Christ also suffered for you, leaving you an example for you to follow in His steps, who committed no sin, nor was any deceit found in His mouth; and while being reviled, He did not revile in return; while suffering, He uttered no threats, but kept entrusting Himself to Him who judges righteously.

for those persecuting you that would give you added incentive to be patient?

James connected our ability to wait patiently for the Lord's return with the strengthening of the heart (James 5:8).[189, T76] Paul gave a reason for having our hearts "established" (same Greek word as "strengthened") in light of the return of Christ.[192] What is it?

If James' readers retaliated against those persecuting them, would they be found "without blame in holiness"[192] at the Lord's return? Would you?

HOW NOT TO BE PATIENT

It goes without saying that patience is not demonstrated by retaliation and vengeance against our persecutors. But there is a more subtle form of impatience that we are tempted to give in to when suffering: grumbling against one another. For instance, there may be other Christians nearby who are undergoing none of the persecution or discomfort we are. Or perhaps others are in our same situation but are suffering less—for whatever reason. Finally, we may simply allow our discomfort to produce carnal attitudes and actions against fellow believers. Any or all of these may result in our "complaining" about our circumstances by taking it out on others (James 5:9).[189]

What is the motivation for refraining from this kind of carnality (verse 9)?[189]

The same Lord whose return will bring justice for the persecuted will also judge Christians whose carnal actions unnecessarily hurt others within the body of Christ.

BRINGING IT HOME

1. The doctrine of the nearness of the return of Christ is a double-edged doctrine, one that comforts and warns at the same time. It comforts us with the knowledge that unde-served suffering will end with the Lord's return, and it warns us not to bring undeserved suffering upon others.

   Is there a situation, large or small, in which you are suf-fering undeservedly at the hands of another person? What does this passage contribute to your ability to endure with patience instead of frustration?

   What does God desire for the one(s) causing your suffer-ing? What is the best way for you to cooperate with and facilitate God's desires for that person(s)?

2. Are you, through carnal complaining, making life diffi-cult for a fellow believer? What would happen to you if Christ, as Judge, returned today? What should that real-ity motivate you to do?

3. What is your ultimate responsibility to "all men," that is, to both those who persecute you and those whom you might be tempted to hurt by your complaining (see Romans 12:18)?[193]

STUDY TECHNIQUES:[T76]

BUTTRESS YOUR FAITH—The word James used in 5:8 for "strengthening" one's heart (*sterizo*) was used in classical Greek to describe the building of a buttress on the outside wall of a building to strengthen its ability to hold weight and withstand pressure. This is a perfect illustration for James' figura-tive use of the word. What can we do to strengthen our hearts so as to bear not only a present situation of suffering but also to bear the searching gaze of the Lord as He evaluates our works upon His return? Prayer, Bible study, accountability, and fellowship with other believers serves the former, while righteousness, obedience, and holy living serve the latter.

DAILY READING

Read 1 Peter 2:20-23.[194] Mark all the parallels between Christ and the life James exhorted his readers (including us) to live while suffer-ing undeservedly.

DAY 3

HOW TO ENDURE LIKE JOB AND THE PROPHETS

[195] **ACTS 7**
52 Which one of the prophets did your fathers not persecute?

[196] **LUKE 11**
48 "You are witnesses and approve the deeds of your fathers; because it was they who killed them, and you build their tombs."

[197] **2 TIMOTHY 3**
12 All who desire to live godly in Christ Jesus will be persecuted.

[198] **JOB 1**
20-22 Job arose and tore his robe and shaved his head, and he fell to the ground and worshiped. He said, "Naked I came from my mother's womb, and naked I shall return there. The LORD gave and the LORD has taken away. Blessed be the name of the LORD." Through all this Job did not sin nor did he blame God.

[199] **JOB 2**
9-10 [Job's] wife said to him, "Do you still hold fast your integrity? Curse God and die!" But he said to her, "You speak as one of the foolish women speaks. Shall we indeed accept good from God and not accept adversity?" In all this Job did not sin with his lips.

[200] **JOB 3**
1,26 Job opened his mouth and cursed the day of his birth. . . .
"I am not at ease, nor am I quiet, and I am not at rest, but turmoil comes."

James wanted his Christian brothers and sisters to do two things when they found themselves persecuted without cause: be patient and persevere.[177] To illustrate these two goals, he began by citing farmers as an example of patience in 5:7. In the present verses (5:10-12), he added perseverance to patience. The prophets of the Old Testament were examples of patience; Job, an example of perseverance.

Finally—"above all"—James condemned the use of oaths (promises to God) as a vehicle for escaping suffering. He left no "out" for the suffering believer. He was returning to the theme mentioned in chapter 1 of his letter, that for suffering and testing to produce perseverance (1:3), we must persevere! One way we know we have failed God's test is when we will do anything to escape it.

PATIENT PROPHETS

God's prophets in the Old Testament were His spokesmen, His mouthpieces on earth. That fact makes James' words here more than a history lesson for the believer today. (For verses 10-12, see appendix A.)

Which of God's prophets in the Old Testament escaped being persecuted for saying what God wanted said (Acts 7:52)?[195]

What happened to the prophet Jeremiah?

• Jeremiah 20:2: Pashhur had Jeremiah the prophet beaten and put him in the stocks that were at the upper Benjamin Gate, which was by the house of the Lord.

• Jeremiah 32:3: Zedekiah king of Judah had shut [Jeremiah] up, saying, "Why do you prophesy, saying, 'Thus says the LORD,' Behold, I am about to give this city into the hand of the king of Babylon, and he will take it"?

• Jeremiah 38:6: They took Jeremiah and cast him into the cistern of Malchijah the king's son, which was in the court of the guardhouse; and they let Jeremiah down with ropes. Now in the cistern there was no water but only mud, and Jeremiah sank into the mud.

What happened to many of the prophets of the Old Testament (Luke 11:48)?[196]

Read Jesus' famous last commission to His disciples (and to us):

> Jesus came up and spoke to them, saying, "All authority has been given to Me in heaven and on earth. Go therefore and make disciples of all the nations, baptizing them in the name of the Father and the Son and the Holy Spirit, teaching them to observe all that I commanded you; and lo, I am with you always, even to the end of the age." (Matthew 28:18-20)

Given these words of Jesus, in what way is every Christian, while not a prophet in the Old Testament sense, nevertheless called on to be a spokesperson for God?

Next, read the conclusion to Jesus' famous Beatitudes:

> "Blessed are you when people insult you and persecute you, and falsely say all kinds of evil against you because of Me. Rejoice and be glad, for your reward in heaven is great; for in the same way they persecuted the prophets who were before you." (Matthew 5:11-12)

What does Jesus' use of "when" instead of "if" in verse 11 suggest to you? Why should you rejoice when you are persecuted as a believer?

The prophets are examples to the believer today because of their facing persecution without bitterness toward God or rebellion against His purposes for them.

STUDY TECHNIQUES:[T77]
PATIENCE AND PERSEVERANCE—The Greek verb for "be patient" (*makrothumeo*) and its corresponding noun, "patience" (*makrothumia*), suggest an attitude of self-restraint, of putting distance between oneself and anger (*makros* = distant, long; *thumos* = anger, rage). James suggested that his readers restrain themselves and not give in to anger or rage toward their wealthy oppressors. In James 5:11 the focus switches from patience to perseverance or endurance (*hupomeno* = to endure, persevere; *hupomone* = perseverance, endurance). Perseverance engages the opposition—not personally, but so as not to be defeated by the struggle). Patience is self-control, not allowing the dissipation of strength and energy in fruitless endeavor, while perseverance channels that energy into remaining strong and resolute until the conflict is over.

CROSS REFERENCES:[T78]
UNDESERVED SUFFERING—Job did not know why he suffered; he only knew (or at least felt) that he had not sinned. In the New Testament, the most thorough exposition of how to suffer when innocent is found in 1 Peter. First, in 1 Peter 2:18-25 employees (actually slaves) are asked to follow the example of Christ, who suffered though innocent. He was patient, entrusting Himself to God, who judges justly (compare James 5:7). Then in 1 Peter 3:8-17 sufferers are cautioned not to seek vengeance but respectfully to give an answer for the hope within them. Finally, in 1 Peter 4:12-19 believers are reminded that it is a privilege and joy to participate in the sufferings of Christ. For anyone who suffers without good cause, 1 Peter is the book to digest.

[201] JOB 12

1-3 Job responded, "Truly then you are the people, and with you wisdom will die! But I have intelligence as well as you; I am not inferior to you. And who does not know such things as these?"

[202] JOB 13

3-4 I would speak to the Almighty, and I desire to argue with God. But you smear with lies; you are all worthless physicians.

[203] JOB 13

15 Though [God] slay me, I will hope in Him. Nevertheless I will argue my ways before Him.

[204] JOB 16

1-3 Job answered, "I have heard many such things; sorry comforters are you all. Is there no limit to windy words? Or what plagues you that you answer?"

[205] JOB 21

4 As for me, is my complaint to man? And why should I not be impatient?

[206] JOB 19

25-27 As for me, I know that my Redeemer lives, and at the last He will take His stand on the earth. Even after my skin is destroyed, yet from my flesh I shall see God; whom I myself shall behold, and whom my eyes will see and not another. My heart faints within me!

They accepted suffering as the outcome of their ministry—part of their job description. Who else should recognize that persecution and suffering are part of their marching orders and prepare not to complain or rebel against it?[197]

IMPATIENT (BUT PERSEVERING) JOB

If patience is a passive acceptance of suffering, perseverance is an active standing in the face of it. Both are needed by the believer, James said. The prophets were patient, but Job, in spite of the time-honored "patience of Job" label, was anything but patient. He was an impatient, but persevering, sufferer.[T78]

Each of the following verses gives evidence of either Job's impatience or his perseverance. Note the evidence for each:

	Impatience	Perseverance
Job 1:20-22[198]		
Job 2:9-10[199]		
Job 3:1,26[200]		
Job 12:1-3[201]		
Job 13:3-4[202]		
Job 13:15[203]		
Job 16:1-3[204]		
Job 21:4[205]		

Both patience and perseverance are desired qualities. While patience is willing to rest in a larger plan, perseverance continues to search for closure, knowing that is found ultimately in the justice of God. How is Job 19:25-27[206] a clear statement of Job's ultimate attitude of perseverance?

James again picked up a theme from chapter 1—joy and blessedness in times of suffering. What is the blessed condition of the person who perseveres (James 1:4)?[31]

SWEARING OFF OATHS

Have you ever made promises to God when in a dire situation? Lots of soldiers have in wartime—it's why they say there are no atheists in foxholes! James warned his readers against the trivial use of oaths and promises in God's name. Perhaps his readers were trying to avoid what God had planned by making an oath (a promise) to Him: "Lord, if You will let this suffering pass, I promise to give the church a tenth of my income forever!"[T79]

James echoed almost verbatim the words of Jesus on this subject (Matthew 5:33-37; see appendix A). Compare Jesus' last word (making illegitimate oaths is "evil," verse 37) with James' ("you will be condemned," James 5:12). Also, read about Jesus' temptation by Satan in the wilderness (Luke 4:1-13; see appendix A). Describe a time when you were tempted to make a promise to God in exchange for the end of your suffering.

BRINGING IT HOME

1. When it comes to suffering unjustly, are you more like the prophets (patient) or like Job (impatient but persevering)? Can you give an example or two that documents your "suffering style"?

2. Since both patience and perseverance are godly characteristics, the absence of either can have negative consequences. Thinking about the trait you are not strongest in, how have you seen negative results from a lack of that trait?

3. Have you ever made a vow to God when in a situation of suffering or discomfort? Did you keep it? How does Ecclesiastes 5:5 ("It is better that you should not vow than that you should vow and not pay") give guidance consistent with James' teaching about the casual use of vows?

HISTORY & CULTURE:[T79]

GOOD OATHS—James' prohibition against oaths refers to a practice that had degenerated from serious to trivial in Israel. An oath was used to call someone as a witness that you would keep your promise, or to say yourself, "I promise that what I am saying is true." God swore an oath to Abraham (Hebrews 6:13), prophetically to Christ (Psalm 110:4), and to David (Psalm 89:35-37). Jesus swore before Caiaphas (Matthew 26:63-64), and Paul swore on several occasions (Romans 1:9; 9:1; 2 Corinthians 1:18; Galatians 1:20). Oaths were used to establish a basis for trust in disputes (Exodus 22:11). The oaths that James condemned were trivializing a serious process, bordering on taking the Lord's name in vain (Exodus 20:7). A Christian's every word should not need an oath to validate it. Yes should mean yes, and no should mean no.

DAILY READING

Read 1 Peter 4:12-19 (see appendix A). Mark all the parallel principles you find that support what James presented on suffering unjustly.

DAY 4

WHY YOU SHOULD PRAY NO MATTER WHAT

[207]**MATTHEW 26**

36,39 Jesus came with them to a place called Gethsemane, and said to His disciples, "Sit here while I go over there and pray." . . . And He went a little beyond them, and fell on His face and prayed, saying, "My Father, if it is possible, let this cup pass from Me; yet not as I will, but as You will."

[208]**JAMES 5**

13-15 Is anyone among you suffering? Then he must pray. Is anyone cheerful? He is to sing praises. Is anyone among you sick? Then he must call for the elders of the church and they are to pray over him, anointing him with oil in the name of the Lord; and the prayer offered in faith will restore the one who is sick, and the Lord will raise him up, and if he has committed sins, they will be forgiven him.

While it's not always true, writers and speakers have a natural tendency to summarize, to conclude, to bring closure, or to give final words of instruction or advice when they near the end of a presentation. We know this, and so we often jump ahead to the last chapter or paragraph of something we're reading in order to get to the "bottom line" (or to find out "who done it" in the mystery we're reading).

As James brought his letter to a close, you can almost hear the wheels of his mind turning over as he formulates his conclusion. His readers were in a tough situation—dispersed from their homes, persecuted by the powerful, tempted to live more like those they were around than like Christ, quarreling and sniping at each other, and growing impatient with God's plan for their lives. James knew that for any Christian—first-century or twenty-first century—there is a central element in the Christian life: prayer.

WHY PRAYER?

The human life in the natural realm needs a number of things to be healthy: oxygen, food, rest, exercise, and water. Which is the most important? If we follow the general rule that a person can survive forty days without food, four days without water, but only four minutes without oxygen, then we might conclude that oxygen is the most important.

What about the spiritual life? What are the essential components to staying spiritually healthy?

Why, in your opinion, did James focus on prayer in his final words as opposed to any of the other important elements? Why is prayer the "air" of the spiritual life?

Think of it this way: If you are all alone in a desperate situation, what is the one thing you can always do? What did Jesus choose to do in the most desperate hour of His life?[207]

Prayer is not only the most basic of the spiritual disciplines (no other tools, resources, or people needed), but it puts us in touch with the only Person who can truly affect the situation we're in—by changing either the situation or us. For millennia, prayer has been the means for the troubled soul to reach out to its Creator God for help, for comfort, for answers to life's biggest questions (see Psalm 25:1-7 in appendix A). For James to focus on prayer at the end of his letter is a sign of his own maturity and depth of understanding.

REASONS TO PRAY

There are a multitude of reasons to pray, but James mentioned three. What are they, and why do you think he mentioned these three to his readers?[208, T80]

1.

2.

3.

Especially compelling is James' exhortation for Christians to pray when they are "cheerful" (verse 13).[208] Why is this reminder so important for people in difficult circumstances?[T81]

James gave extended effort to discussing prayers for the sick. To grasp the "big picture" of what James was prescribing, list as many of the who, what, when, where, why, and how elements of prayers for the sick as you can find in verses 14-15:[208, T82]

Strangely, prayer for the sick as prescribed by James is missing in many contemporary churches. Why do you think that is true?

STUDY TECHNIQUES:[T80]

PRAYER IN PERSECUTION—Language often provides the link we need to connect an author's thoughts. We know that James' exhortation to prayer is tied to his readers' suffering because of the words he used. In 5:10 James used the noun *kakopatheia* for the suffering the prophets endured, which he used as an example for believers to imitate. Then, in 5:13, he used the verb form of the same word, *kakopatheo*, when he asked, "Is anyone among you suffering?" So, his words about patience in suffering (5:7-11) are followed by words about prayer in suffering (5:13-18). Patience and prayer—biblical advice on how to endure when you suffer.

POINT OF INTEREST:[T81]

PRAYERS OF PRAISE—Unfortunately, prayers of praise, arising out of hearts filled with blessing and joy, are among the last to leave our lips. Understandably, the press of daily life, and its multitudes of needs, cause us to pour out our petitions ahead of our praise. But think about it—aren't there many more hours in the day when we are blessed than when we are pressed? It's not that we don't have many reasons and opportunities to praise God; it's just that we don't take time to do it. Ranging from Moses and Miriam's song of praise for the exodus from Egypt (Exodus 15:1-21) to the song of praise of the twenty-four elders in heaven (Revelation 11:15-18), the Bible is filled with people who stopped to give praise to God for His goodness. What do you have to thank God for today? Perhaps you could pause, even now, and offer a prayer of praise to Him.

RIGHTEOUSNESS AND PRAYER

Some Christian communities have incorrectly made a direct correlation between righteousness (or the lack of it) and prayer, especially in the case of sickness. What connection did James make at the end of verse 15 (note the word "if")?[208]

Under the Old Covenant, Israel was told that there would be a definite connection between their attitude toward sin and their physical health.[T83] While that connection has not been repeated in as direct a way to the church, it is clear that the believer's righteousness is an important variable when it comes to answered prayer. Note the kinds of unrighteousness that can hinder our prayers to God:

- Mark 11:24[209] (see also James 1:6-7)

- Isaiah 1:15[210] (see also 1 John 3:21-22)

- Proverbs 21:13[211] (see also Luke 6:38)

- 1 Peter 3:7[212]

- Matthew 6:14-15[74] (see also 18:21-35)

- James 4:3[146]

- Psalm 66:18[213] (see also Isaiah 59:2)

What connection do you see between James 4:1-2,11-12; 5:9 (see appendix A) and James 5:16[214]?

In light of what Elijah's prayers accomplished, why do you think James said Elijah was a "man with a nature like ours" (James 5:17)?[214]

---

[209]**MARK 11**

24 "All things for which you pray and ask, believe that you have received them, and they will be granted you."

[210]**ISAIAH 1**

15 "When you spread out your hands in prayer, I will hide My eyes from you; yes, even though you multiply prayers, I will not listen. Your hands are covered with blood."

[211]**PROVERBS 21**

13 He who shuts his ear to the cry of the poor will also cry himself and not be answered.

[212]**1 PETER 3**

7 You husbands . . . , show [your wife] honor as a fellow heir of the grace of life, so that your prayers will not be hindered.

[213]**PSALM 66**

18 If I regard wickedness in my heart, the Lord will not hear.

[214]**JAMES 5**

16-18 Confess your sins to one another, and pray for one another so that you may be healed. The effective prayer of a righteous man can accomplish much. Elijah was a man with a nature like ours, and he prayed earnestly that it would not rain, and it did not rain on the earth for three years and six months. Then he prayed again, and the sky poured rain and the earth produced its fruit.

BRINGING IT HOME

1. Evaluate your own prayer life on the following scale (circle the correct answer):

I rarely, if ever, pray. I know I should, but I can't seem to make it happen.	I mainly pray when I need God's help with a problem or need. I feel guilty only praying then, but it's better than not praying at all.	I pray consistently usually several times per week, about various kinds of things.	I pray daily in my personal devotional time and am keeping up with my prayer life in a journal or other record.	I pray daily, and frequently with groups or my spouse for extended times of prayer for other needs.

2. What are the biggest obstacles to your making progress in prayer? What do you think would help you overcome those obstacles?

3. What is your "Worthiness Quotient"? If Elijah was a person just like us (a sinner saved by grace), and he accomplished great things through prayer, why can't we (James wants to know)? We are usually so conscious of our own unrighteousness that we don't think we are worthy to have our prayers answered by God. And guess what? We're not! Fortunately, though, unrighteous Christians like us have been made righteous by being in Christ (Romans 3:22). And when we do sin, "Jesus Christ the righteous" speaks to the Father on our behalf (1 John 2:1). Therefore, confess your sins—and pray (James 5:16; 1 John 1:9)!

HISTORY & CULTURE:[T82]

ELDERS AND ANOINTING—When James said to "call for the elders," to whom was he referring? In Titus 1:5,7 and Acts 20:17,28, elders and bishops (or overseers) are equated. Different words were used to describe aspects of the same office. The elders in Acts 20:28 were told to "shepherd" (or "pastor") the flock, and 1 Peter 5:1-4 seems to link elders, bishops, and pastors together as being the same person. "Elders" suggest a plurality of leaders, with some who have the gift/office of pastor-teacher (Ephesians 4:11). So James was directing the sick person to call for the leaders of his or her church—regardless of their title—to pray and anoint with oil.

CROSS REFERENCES:[T83]

SIN AND SICKNESS—When Israel entered into a covenantal relationship with God following the Exodus, their health and welfare was to be a sign to the nations of the love and care of their God. If they walked in the covenant and obeyed God, then His blessings would come upon them in every area of life (Deuteronomy 28:1-14). If they chose to disobey God, however, diseases would be one of the evidences of their sin (Deuteronomy 28:21-22,27-28,35,59-61). Whereas God's power was to be made perfect in strength in Israel, His power is now made perfect in weakness in the church (2 Corinthians 12:9). God gives gifts of healing in the church (1 Corinthians 12:28), and sin still affects our health at times (1 Corinthians 11:29-31).

DAILY READING

Read Psalm 32 (see appendix A). Mark the elements of prayer in times of suffering that parallel James' teaching in this section of his letter.

DAY 5

THE WISEST THING YOU COULD EVER DO

[215]**JAMES 5**

19-20 My brethren, if any among you strays from the truth and one turns him back, let him know that he who turns a sinner from the error of his way will save his soul from death and will cover a multitude of sins.

[216]**MATTHEW 18**

12 "If any man has a hundred sheep, and one of them has gone astray, does he not leave the ninety-nine on the mountains and go and search for the one that is straying?"

[217]**ACTS 20**

30-31 From among your own selves men will arise, speaking perverse things, to draw away the disciples after them. Therefore be on the alert, remembering that night and day for a period of three years I did not cease to admonish each one with tears.

[218]**2 TIMOTHY 2**

18 . . . men who have gone astray from the truth saying that the resurrection has already taken place, and they upset the faith of some.

[219]**1 CORINTHIANS 5**

1 It is actually reported that there is immorality among you, and immorality of such a kind as does not exist even among the Gentiles, that someone has his father's wife.

[220]**1 TIMOTHY 1**

19 . . . keeping faith and a good conscience, which some have rejected and suffered shipwreck in regard to their faith.

As we close our study of the letter of James, reviewing its contents helps us understand James' final words (5:19-20).[215] He was trying, long-distance, to provide spiritual and practical guidance—impart wisdom—to a number of Jewish Christians who had been driven from their homes in Jerusalem. We know they were suffering (1:2-4; 5:7-11) at the hands of oppressors (2:6-7; 5:1-6) and were tempted as a result to engage in retaliation or other unseemly behavior (1:13-15,19-20). In general, their lives had taken on a carnal character that, to James, called into question the reality of their profession to be Christians (1:22-25; 2:14-26). Their speech was bitter (1:26; 3:1-12); they were quarreling, fighting, and criticizing one another (4:1-3,11-12); they were catering to their rich oppressors and ignoring their own poor and needy (1:27–2:11); and they had become proud and boastful in their worldliness (4:4-17). When they prayed, it was with impure motives (4:3), but they seemed to have forgotten how to pray at all (5:13-18).

Not a pretty picture from James' perspective. He knew all too well what might happen next in this type of demoralizing situation: Downtrodden, disobedient, and increasingly discouraged church members could begin to leave the faith altogether. It was to prevent this from happening that James penned his final words to the church.

The final message of James to the church was this: "Sheep are prone to wander under the best of circumstances, and they will bolt and run in the face of danger. The wise among you will keep an eye out for the wanderers in the flock. Go after them and bring them back! In doing so you save them from certain death, the natural consequence of their sins."[215]

Christianity is not a solo endeavor; it is a group event. And all the members are responsible for all the others. Therefore, James said, the body should pay close attention to those who were wandering—and bring them back.[T84]

THE WANDERER

It seems clear that James was referring to a professing Christian wandering away from the faith. "Brethren" and "any among you" make this clear. Another way of looking at it is to note the use of the word "strays"—it is the same word Jesus used in describing the stray sheep in Matthew 18:12.[216, T85] What must one first be part of before he or she can stray away?

There are two ways for a believer to wander from the truth (in James' case, the truth was apostolic doctrine being guarded by the leaders of the early church, spread by letters such as James'; in our day, the truth is that contained in the completed Bible). The first is by denying sound doctrine. What did Paul warn the elders of the church at Ephesus about in this regard (Acts 20:30)?[217]

What was his watchword to them (Acts 20:31)?[217]

How did two men named Hymenaeus and Philetus wander from the truth (2 Timothy 2:18)?[218]

The second way for a believer to stray from truth is through immorality. How had this occurred in Corinth (1 Corinthians 5:1)?[219]

What graphic picture did Paul use of a Christian who failed to keep a clear conscience before God (1 Timothy 1:19)?[220]

THE WISE

James called upon the wise in the church to reach out to those who were straying or were tempted to do so. Nowhere is the root meaning of "wise" (skill) more needed than in such an instance as turning a wandering sheep back to the path of life. Make a note of the kinds of wisdom called for by the admonitions in the following verses:

• Matthew 7:5[57]

• Matthew 18:15-20 (see appendix A)

POINT OF INTEREST:[T84]
UNITY AND DIVERSITY — Two metaphors used in Scripture support James' exhortation to seek out and bring back wandering Christians: the flock and the body. In Acts 20, Paul tells the elders of the church in Ephesus to "be on guard for yourselves and for all the flock" because "savage wolves will come in . . . , not sparing the flock" (verses 28-29). Because of the tendency of sheep to wander, and because of the need to keep a sharp eye on each one, a flock is a perfect metaphor for the church. "The body" is mentioned thirteen times in 1 Corinthians 12 alone as Paul used the human body as a picture of the church, the body of Christ. Just as the human body's immune system rallies to the defense of an injured or weak part, so the church must watch out even for its smallest and weakest members. The body especially is a beautiful picture of unity and diversity. Each individual Christian is unique and free to express his or her relationship in a personal way. Yet if that individual part of the body grows weak in faith, the rest of the body as a unit is to be there to strengthen and restore it.

221 GALATIANS 6

9 Let us not lose heart in doing good, for in due time we will reap if we do not grow weary.

222 1 PETER 4

8 Above all, keep fervent in your love for one another, because love covers a multitude of sins.

- Galatians 6:1[167]

- Galatians 6:9[221]

- Ephesians 4:32[76]

- James 4:6[152]

- 1 Peter 4:8[222]

The person seeking to restore a wandering brother or sister may not know for sure whether the person is a genuinely converted individual or not. Granted, James was referring to a person from within the professing, organized church. But that is not a guarantee that the person is genuinely a Christian. He or she may be a professing Christian only and not possess eternal life.

Whether the wanderer is a genuine believer or not, the wise person who goes after that one has saved him or her from death. If the wanderer is not a believer, then he has been saved from eternal death by being confronted with the error of his ways and brought face-to-face with the gospel. If the person is a Christian, then she may have been saved from physical death. There is ample warrant in Scripture for believing that God would allow a path of self-destruction (1 Corinthians 5:5) or even death (1 Corinthians 11:30-32) for a sinning Christian as a form of severe discipline. Either way, a skillful Christian demonstrates abundant wisdom and understanding by leaving "the ninety-nine on the mountains and [going] and [searching] for the one that is straying" (Matthew 18:12).[T86]

BRINGING IT HOME

1. In your Christian experience, have you ever strayed (or been tempted to stray) from the truth? Was your wandering of a doctrinal or a moral nature? What conditions resulted in your vulnerability at that time? Have you made it back to a place of strong faith at this time? How did that happen?

2. Have you witnessed the kind of seeking and restoration that James encouraged at work in the church? If you have personally been involved in such an effort, what were the results? What did you learn about restoring a wanderer? What would you do differently the next time?

3. From your vantage point in the body of Christ, what kinds of "wandering" do you see happening? What types of efforts at restoration do you see taking place? Why do you think the body of Christ has not taken James' exhortation more seriously?

4. No Christian can read all the way through James' letter, as you have now done, without being touched somewhere along the way. All of the five units, corresponding to James' five chapters, are valuable, but see if you can rank all five in terms of their personal helpfulness to your life (1 = the unit that addressed your most pressing needs, and 5 = the unit that addressed needs that are least pressing in your life at this time):

Unit 1: Wisdom in Troubles and Temptation (James 1)
   • Wisdom in trials; temptations _____

Unit 2: Wisdom in Friendships and Faith (James 2)
   • Favoritism; faith that is alive and that works _____

Unit 3: Wisdom in Taming the Tongue (James 3)
   • The tongue; earthly versus heavenly wisdom _____

Unit 4: Wisdom for the Humble and the Hopeful (James 4)
   • Dangers of pride; how to humble yourself _____

Unit 5: Wisdom in Prosperity, Patience, and Prayer (James 5)
   • Patience and endurance; righteous prayer _____

5. A good way to review a book of the Bible after studying it in detail (especially a short book like James) is to reread it several times straight through, in one sitting. This has the advantage of tying together the individual parts you have studied in detail. Enter the dates in the spaces below to record your post-GUIDEBOOK readings of James:

   Reading 1: _____
   Reading 2: _____
   Reading 3: _____

CROSS REFERENCES:[T85]

WANDERING SHEEP—A passage in Ezekiel is an important corollary to James' words because it reveals God's commitment to caring for each sheep in the flock:

> Those who are sickly you have not strengthened, the diseased you have not healed, the broken you have not bound up, the scattered you have not brought back, nor have you sought for the lost. . . . They were scattered . . . and they became food for every beast of the field and were scattered. My flock wandered [and] . . . was scattered over all the surface of the earth, and there was no one to search or seek for them. (Ezekiel 34:4-6)

James saw the vulnerable position the dispersed church was in and wanted to prevent even a single sheep from straying—something that is obviously a priority with God (Luke 15:3-7).

POINT OF INTEREST:[T86]

GOD'S WILL FOR THE WANDERER—The apostle Peter told us clearly what the will of God is concerning those who have wandered from the truth: He does not wish "for any to perish but for all to come to repentance" (2 Peter 3:9). Whether a person needs to repent as an unbeliever or a believer, repentance is the will of God. If the church does not go and plead with those needing to repent, then we only add to the number of those who are outside of His will. We become the ones needing to repent.

DAILY READING

Read Ezekiel 34 (see appendix A). Mark all the verses that indicate how concerned God is for those sheep who may wander, and the priority He places on bringing them back.

To the leader: On a flipchart or marker board, reproduce the scale from the first item of "Bringing It Home" in unit 5, day 4 (page 133). If you collected prayers in envelopes during unit 1's Sharing the Journey session, distribute these to their owners at the end of this session.

1. James had some harsh words of warning for the ungodly rich: They would lose their much-prized wealth. They deserved judgment because of their mistreatment of the righteous poor.
   - How do the wealthy and powerful in our day sometimes treat "the little people" unjustly?
   - What is one way you have been mistreated by someone in a position of power over you? How did it feel? What effect did the experience have on your spiritual life?

2. Addressing those enduring persecution, James urged them to wait patiently for the coming of the Lord.
   - Rate your patience in general. On a scale of 1 to 10 (1 meaning "I go crazy when forced to wait for anything," and 10 meaning "I can wait forever if I have to"), how patient are you?
   - When you're being treated unjustly, is it easier or harder for you to be patient? Why?
   - How does the knowledge that those who mistreat you will be judged by God (whether when the Lord comes back or after their death) affect how you respond to the mistreatment? How does the knowledge that you, yourself, will be judged by God affect how you respond to the mistreatment?

3. The prophets in general, and Job in particular, provide encouraging examples that one can endure suffering. And in the midst of our suffering, we should remember not to make trivial oaths in God's name.
   - In addition to biblical examples like Jeremiah and Job, who else provides a positive example for you of how to endure suffering? (Think of persons in history or in your own life.)
   - Have you ever made a vow to God when in a situation of suffering or discomfort? If so, what was it? Did you keep it? How do you feel about it as you look back now?

4. James commended prayer in every situation. For example, the sick ought to seek the prayer and anointing of church elders for healing. Prayer brings down the power of God.
   - Mark on the scale from "Bringing It Home" in day 4 the frequency with which you pray. Do you find it easier to pray when things are going well or when they are not? Why do you think that is?
   - Is the anointing with oil of the sick something that churches should be doing today? Why or why not?
   - Do you ever confess your sins to a fellow believer? If you like to ham it up, join with a fellow ham to perform two role-plays for the group: In the first, act out a confession of sin in which the two of you handle the situation unwisely (perhaps the one confessing is too explicit and the one listening laughs or criticizes or gossips); in the second, replay the scene but handle the situation in a wise and more godly way.
   - Tell your favorite story of answered prayer.

5. The one who turns a spiritual wanderer back to the truth is doing a very great thing indeed.
   - In your experience, what sorts of things cause people to wander from the truth of the gospel?

- Andrew and Deb became quite involved in their new church when they moved to town eight months ago, and they seemed like faithful Christians. But lately they have all but stopped attending church meetings and they've found new friends in their places of work and their neighborhood. Their church friends, Jim and Karen, have discovered that Andrew and Deb are no longer attending church anywhere and don't seem to mind not praying or worshiping or learning about Scripture.
- If Jim and Karen wanted to try to pull their friends back into Christ's orbit, what steps could they take?
- What one thing that you learned about the book of James during the five sessions of this study stands out in your mind the most right now? What do you most want to take away from this study?

Close in prayer, thanking God for the training in wisdom He provided for us in the book of James. Ask for His grace to help all group members in their present and future trials. In addition, ask for grace to live a life of steadily growing wisdom, skillfully making your faith manifest in what you do and say.

Appendix A—
Scripture Readings

Genesis 15

1 The word of the LORD came to Abram in a vision, saying, "Do not fear, Abram, I am a shield to you; your reward shall be very great."

2 Abram said, "O Lord GOD, what will You give me, since I am childless, and the heir of my house is Eliezer of Damascus?"

3 And Abram said, "Since You have given no offspring to me, one born in my house is my heir."

4 Then behold, the word of the LORD came to him, saying, "This man will not be your heir; but one who will come forth from your own body, he shall be your heir."

5 And He took him outside and said, "Now look toward the heavens, and count the stars, if you are able to count them." And He said to him, "So shall your descendants be."

6 Then he believed in the LORD; and He reckoned it to him as righteousness.

Genesis 22

1 Now it came about after these things, that God tested Abraham, and said to him, "Abraham!" And he said, "Here I am."

2 He said, "Take now your son, your only son, whom you love, Isaac, and go to the land of Moriah, and offer him there as a burnt offering on one of the mountains of which I will tell you."

3 So Abraham rose early in the morning and saddled his donkey, and took two of his young men with him and Isaac his son; and he split wood for the burnt offering, and arose and went to the place of which God had told him.

4 On the third day Abraham raised his eyes and saw the place from a distance.

5 Abraham said to his young men, "Stay here with the donkey, and I and the lad will go over there; and we will worship and return to you."

6 Abraham took the wood of the burnt offering and laid it on Isaac his son, and he took in his hand the fire and the knife. So the two of them walked on together.

7 Isaac spoke to Abraham his father and said,

"My father!" And he said, "Here I am, my son." And he said, "Behold, the fire and the wood, but where is the lamb for the burnt offering?"

8 Abraham said, "God will provide for Himself the lamb for the burnt offering, my son." So the two of them walked on together.

9 Then they came to the place of which God had told him; and Abraham built the altar there and arranged the wood, and bound his son Isaac and laid him on the altar, on top of the wood.

10 Abraham stretched out his hand and took the knife to slay his son.

11 But the angel of the LORD called to him from heaven and said, "Abraham, Abraham!" And he said, "Here I am."

12 He said, "Do not stretch out your hand against the lad, and do nothing to him; for now I know that you fear God, since you have not withheld your son, your only son, from Me."

13 Then Abraham raised his eyes and looked, and behold, behind him a ram caught in the thicket by his horns; and Abraham went and took the ram and offered him up for a burnt offering in the place of his son.

14 Abraham called the name of that place The LORD Will Provide, as it is said to this day, "In the mount of the LORD it will be provided."

15 Then the angel of the LORD called to Abraham a second time from heaven,

16 and said, "By Myself I have sworn, declares the LORD, because you have done this thing and have not withheld your son, your only son,

17 indeed I will greatly bless you, and I will greatly multiply your seed as the stars of the heavens and as the sand which is on the seashore; and your seed shall possess the gate of their enemies.

18 In your seed all the nations of the earth shall be blessed, because you have obeyed My voice."

1 Kings 3

16 Two women who were harlots came to the king and stood before him.

17 The one woman said, "Oh, my lord, this

woman and I live in the same house; and I gave birth to a child while she was in the house.

18 It happened on the third day after I gave birth, that this woman also gave birth to a child, and we were together. There was no stranger with us in the house, only the two of us in the house.

19 This woman's son died in the night, because she lay on it.

20 So she arose in the middle of the night and took my son from beside me while your maidservant slept, and laid him in her bosom, and laid her dead son in my bosom.

21 When I rose in the morning to nurse my son, behold, he was dead; but when I looked at him carefully in the morning, behold, he was not my son, whom I had borne."

22 Then the other woman said, "No! For the living one is my son, and the dead one is your son." But the first woman said, "No! For the dead one is your son, and the living one is my son." Thus they spoke before the king.

23 Then the king said, "The one says, 'This is my son who is living, and your son is the dead one'; and the other says, 'No! For your son is the dead one, and my son is the living one.'"

24 The king said, "Get me a sword." So they brought a sword before the king.

25 The king said, "Divide the living child in two, and give half to the one and half to the other."

26 Then the woman whose child was the living one spoke to the king, for she was deeply stirred over her son and said, "Oh, my lord, give her the living child, and by no means kill him." But the other said, "He shall be neither mine nor yours; divide him!"

27 Then the king said, "Give the first woman the living child, and by no means kill him. She is his mother."

28 When all Israel heard of the judgment which the king had handed down, they feared the king, for they saw that the wisdom of God was in him to administer justice.

PSALM 25

1 To You, O LORD, I lift up my soul.

2 O my God, in You I trust, do not let me be ashamed; do not let my enemies exult over me.

3 Indeed, none of those who wait for You will be ashamed; those who deal treacherously without cause will be ashamed.

4 Make me know Your ways, O LORD; teach me Your paths.

5 Lead me in Your truth and teach me, for You are the God of my salvation; for You I wait all the day.

6 Remember, O LORD, Your compassion and Your lovingkindnesses, for they have been from of old.

7 Do not remember the sins of my youth or my transgressions; according to Your lovingkindness remember me, for Your goodness' sake, O LORD.

PSALM 32

1 How blessed is he whose transgression is forgiven, whose sin is covered!

2 How blessed is the man to whom the Lord does not impute iniquity, and in whose spirit there is no deceit!

3 When I kept silent about my sin, my body wasted away through my groaning all day long.

4 For day and night Your hand was heavy upon me; my vitality was drained away as with the fever heat of summer. Selah.

5 I acknowledged my sin to You, and my iniquity I did not hide; I said, "I will confess my transgressions to the LORD"; and You forgave the guilt of my sin. Selah.

6 Therefore, let everyone who is godly pray to You in a time when You may be found; surely in a flood of great waters they will not reach him.

7 You are my hiding place; You preserve me from trouble; You surround me with songs of deliverance. Selah.

8 I will instruct you and teach you in the way which you should go; I will counsel you with My eye upon you.

9 Do not be as the horse or as the mule which have no understanding, whose trappings include bit and bridle to hold them in check, otherwise they will not come near to you.

10 Many are the sorrows of the wicked, but he who trusts in the Lord, lovingkindness shall surround him.

11 Be glad in the LORD and rejoice, you righteous ones; and shout for joy, all you who are upright in heart.

PROVERBS 1

20 Wisdom shouts in the street, she lifts her voice in the square;

21 at the head of the noisy streets she cries out; at the entrance of the gates in the city she utters her sayings:

22 "How long, O naive ones, will you love being simple-minded? And scoffers delight themselves in scoffing and fools hate knowledge?

23 Turn to my reproof, behold, I will pour out my spirit on you; I will make my words known to you.

24 Because I called and you refused, I stretched out my hand and no one paid attention;

25 and you neglected all my counsel and did not want my reproof;

26 I will also laugh at your calamity; I will mock when your dread comes,

27 when your dread comes like a storm and your calamity comes like a whirlwind, when distress and anguish come upon you.

28 Then they will call on me, but I will not answer; they will seek me diligently but they will not find me,

29 because they hated knowledge and did not choose the fear of the Lord.

30 They would not accept my counsel, they spurned all my reproof.

31 So they shall eat of the fruit of their own way and be satiated with their own devices.

32 For the waywardness of the naive will kill them, and the complacency of fools will destroy them.

33 But he who listens to me shall live securely and will be at ease from the dread of evil."

PROVERBS 2

1 My son, if you will receive my words and treasure my commandments within you,

2 make your ear attentive to wisdom, incline your heart to understanding;

3 for if you cry for discernment, lift your voice for understanding;

4 if you seek her as silver and search for her as for hidden treasures;

5 then you will discern the fear of the LORD and discover the knowledge of God.

6 For the LORD gives wisdom; from His mouth come knowledge and understanding.

7 He stores up sound wisdom for the upright; He is a shield to those who walk in integrity,

8 guarding the paths of justice, and He preserves the way of His godly ones.

PROVERBS 4

1 Hear, O sons, the instruction of a father, and give attention that you may gain understanding,

2 for I give you sound teaching; do not abandon my instruction.

3 When I was a son to my father, tender and the only son in the sight of my mother,

4 then he taught me and said to me, "Let your heart hold fast my words; Keep my commandments and live;

5 Acquire wisdom! Acquire understanding! Do not forget nor turn away from the words of my mouth.

6 Do not forsake her, and she will guard you; love her, and she will watch over you.

7 The beginning of wisdom is: Acquire wisdom; and with all your acquiring, get understanding.

8 Prize her, and she will exalt you; she will honor you if you embrace her.

9 She will place on your head a garland of grace; she will present you with a crown of beauty."

10 Hear, my son, and accept my sayings and the years of your life will be many.

11 I have directed you in the way of wisdom; I have led you in upright paths.

12 When you walk, your steps will not be impeded; and if you run, you will not stumble.

13 Take hold of instruction; do not let go. Guard her, for she is your life.

14 Do not enter the path of the wicked and do not proceed in the way of evil men.

15 Avoid it, do not pass by it; turn away from it and pass on.

16 For they cannot sleep unless they do evil; and they are robbed of sleep unless they make someone stumble.

17 For they eat the bread of wickedness and drink the wine of violence.

18 But the path of the righteous is like the light of dawn, that shines brighter and brighter until the full day.

19 The way of the wicked is like darkness; they do not know over what they stumble.

20 My son, give attention to my words; incline your ear to my sayings.

21 Do not let them depart from your sight; keep them in the midst of your heart.

22 For they are life to those who find them and health to all their body.

23 Watch over your heart with all diligence, for from it flow the springs of life.

24 Put away from you a deceitful mouth and put devious speech far from you.

25 Let your eyes look directly ahead and let your gaze be fixed straight in front of you.

26 Watch the path of your feet and all your ways will be established.

27 Do not turn to the right nor to the left; turn your foot from evil.

PROVERBS 8

22 The LORD possessed me at the beginning of His way, before His works of old.

23 From everlasting I was established, from the beginning, from the earliest times of the earth.

24 When there were no depths I was brought forth, when there were no springs abounding with water.

25 Before the mountains were settled, before the hills I was brought forth;

26 while He had not yet made the earth and the fields, nor the first dust of the world.

27 When He established the heavens, I was there, when He inscribed a circle on the face of the deep,

28 when He made firm the skies above, when the springs of the deep became fixed,

29 when He set for the sea its boundary so that the water would not transgress His command, when He marked out the foundations of the earth;

30 then I was beside Him, as a master workman; and I was daily His delight,

31 rejoicing always before Him, rejoicing in the world, His earth, and having my delight in the sons of men.

ECCLESIASTES 5

1 Guard your steps as you go to the house of God and draw near to listen rather than to offer the sacrifice of fools; for they do not know they are doing evil.

2 Do not be hasty in word or impulsive in thought to bring up a matter in the presence of God. For God is in heaven and you are on the earth; therefore let your words be few.

3 For the dream comes through much effort and the voice of a fool through many words.

4 When you make a vow to God, do not be late in paying it; for He takes no delight in fools. Pay what you vow!

5 It is better that you should not vow than that you should vow and not pay.

6 Do not let your speech cause you to sin and do not say in the presence of the messenger of God that it was a mistake. Why should God be angry on account of your voice and destroy the work of your hands?

7 For in many dreams and in many words there is emptiness. Rather, fear God.

EZEKIEL 34

1 The word of the LORD came to me saying,

2 "Son of man, prophesy against the shepherds of Israel. Prophesy and say to those shepherds, 'Thus says the Lord GOD, "Woe, shepherds of Israel who have been feeding themselves! Should not the shepherds feed the flock?

3 You eat the fat and clothe yourselves with the wool, you slaughter the fat sheep without feeding the flock.

4 Those who are sickly you have not strengthened, the diseased you have not healed, the broken you have not bound up, the scattered you have not brought back, nor have you sought for the lost; but with force and with severity you have dominated them.

5 They were scattered for lack of a shepherd, and they became food for every beast of the field and were scattered.

6 My flock wandered through all the mountains and on every high hill; My flock was scattered over all the surface of the earth, and there was no one to search or seek for them." ' "

7 Therefore, you shepherds, hear the word of the LORD:

8 "As I live," declares the Lord GOD, "surely because My flock has become a prey, My flock has even become food for all the beasts of the field for lack of a shepherd, and My shepherds did not search for My flock, but rather the shepherds fed themselves and did not feed My flock;

9 therefore, you shepherds, hear the word of the LORD:

10 'Thus says the Lord GOD, "Behold, I am against the shepherds, and I will demand My sheep from them and make them cease from feeding sheep. So the shepherds will not feed themselves anymore, but I will deliver My flock from their mouth, so that they will not be food for them." ' "

11 For thus says the Lord GOD, "Behold, I Myself will search for My sheep and seek them out.

12 As a shepherd cares for his herd in the day when he is among his scattered sheep, so I will care for My sheep and will deliver them from all the places to which they were scattered on a cloudy and gloomy day.

13 I will bring them out from the peoples and gather them from the countries and bring them to their own land; and I will feed them on the mountains of Israel, by the streams, and in all the inhabited places of the land.

14 I will feed them in a good pasture, and their grazing ground will be on the mountain heights of Israel. There they will lie down on good grazing

ground and feed in rich pasture on the mountains of Israel.

15 I will feed My flock and I will lead them to rest," declares the Lord GOD.

16 "I will seek the lost, bring back the scattered, bind up the broken and strengthen the sick; but the fat and the strong I will destroy. I will feed them with judgment.

17 As for you, My flock, thus says the Lord GOD, 'Behold, I will judge between one sheep and another, between the rams and the male goats.

18 Is it too slight a thing for you that you should feed in the good pasture, that you must tread down with your feet the rest of your pastures? Or that you should drink of the clear waters, that you must foul the rest with your feet?

19 As for My flock, they must eat what you tread down with your feet and drink what you foul with your feet!' "

20 Therefore, thus says the Lord GOD to them, "Behold, I, even I, will judge between the fat sheep and the lean sheep.

21 Because you push with side and with shoulder, and thrust at all the weak with your horns until you have scattered them abroad,

22 therefore, I will deliver My flock, and they will no longer be a prey; and I will judge between one sheep and another.

23 Then I will set over them one shepherd, My servant David, and he will feed them; he will feed them himself and be their shepherd.

24 And I, the LORD, will be their God, and My servant David will be prince among them; I the LORD have spoken.

25 I will make a covenant of peace with them and eliminate harmful beasts from the land so that they may live securely in the wilderness and sleep in the woods.

26 I will make them and the places around My hill a blessing. And I will cause showers to come down in their season; they will be showers of blessing.

27 Also the tree of the field will yield its fruit and the earth will yield its increase, and they will be secure on their land. Then they will know that I am the Lord, when I have broken the bars of their yoke and have delivered them from the hand of those who enslaved them.

28 They will no longer be a prey to the nations, and the beasts of the earth will not devour them; but they will live securely, and no one will make them afraid.

29 I will establish for them a renowned planting place, and they will not again be victims of famine in the land, and they will not endure the insults of the nations anymore.

30 Then they will know that I, the LORD their God, am with them, and that they, the house of Israel, are My people," declares the Lord GOD.

31 "As for you, My sheep, the sheep of My pasture, you are men, and I am your God," declares the Lord GOD.

MATTHEW 5

33 "You have heard that the ancients were told, 'YOU SHALL NOT MAKE FALSE VOWS, BUT SHALL FULFILL YOUR VOWS TO THE LORD.'

34 But I say to you, make no oath at all, either by heaven, for it is the throne of God,

35 or by the earth, for it is the footstool of His feet, or by Jerusalem, for it is THE CITY OF THE GREAT KING.

36 Nor shall you make an oath by your head, for you cannot make one hair white or black.

37 But let your statement be, 'Yes, yes' or 'No, no'; anything beyond these is of evil."

MATTHEW 5

43 "You have heard that it was said, 'YOU SHALL LOVE YOUR NEIGHBOR and hate your enemy.'

44 But I say to you, love your enemies and pray for those who persecute you,

45 so that you may be sons of your Father who is in heaven; for He causes His sun to rise on the evil and the good, and sends rain on the righteous and the unrighteous.

46 For if you love those who love you, what reward do you have? Do not even the tax collectors do the same?

47 If you greet only your brothers, what more are you doing than others? Do not even the Gentiles do the same?

48 Therefore you are to be perfect, as your heavenly Father is perfect."

MATTHEW 6

1 "Beware of practicing your righteousness before men to be noticed by them; otherwise you have no reward with your Father who is in heaven.

2 "So when you give to the poor, do not sound a trumpet before you, as the hypocrites do in the synagogues and in the streets, so that they may be honored by men. Truly I say to you, they have their reward in full.

3 But when you give to the poor, do not let your left hand know what your right hand is doing,

4 so that your giving will be in secret; and your Father who sees what is done in secret will reward you.

5 When you pray, you are not to be like the hypocrites; for they love to stand and pray in the synagogues and on the street corners so that they may be seen by men. Truly I say to you, they have their reward in full.

6 But you, when you pray, go into your inner room, close your door and pray to your Father who is in secret, and your Father who sees what is done in secret will reward you.

7 And when you are praying, do not use meaningless repetition as the Gentiles do, for they suppose that they will be heard for their many words.

8 So do not be like them; for your Father knows what you need before you ask Him.

9 "Pray, then, in this way: 'Our Father who is in heaven, Hallowed be Your name.

10 Your kingdom come. Your will be done, On earth as it is in heaven.

11 Give us this day our daily bread.

12 And forgive us our debts, as we also have forgiven our debtors.

13 And do not lead us into temptation, but deliver us from evil. For Yours is the kingdom and the power and the glory forever. Amen.'

14 For if you forgive others for their transgressions, your heavenly Father will also forgive you.

15 But if you do not forgive others, then your Father will not forgive your transgressions.

16 "Whenever you fast, do not put on a gloomy face as the hypocrites do, for they neglect their appearance so that they will be noticed by men when they are fasting. Truly I say to you, they have their reward in full.

17 But you, when you fast, anoint your head and wash your face

18 so that your fasting will not be noticed by men, but by your Father who is in secret; and your Father who sees what is done in secret will reward you."

MATTHEW 6

25 "I say to you, do not be worried about your life, as to what you will eat or what you will drink; nor for your body, as to what you will put on. Is not life more than food, and the body more than clothing?

26 Look at the birds of the air, that they do not sow, nor reap nor gather into barns, and yet your heavenly Father feeds them. Are you not worth much more than they?

27 And who of you by being worried can add a single hour to his life?

28 And why are you worried about clothing? Observe how the lilies of the field grow; they do not toil nor do they spin,

29 yet I say to you that not even Solomon in all his glory clothed himself like one of these.

30 But if God so clothes the grass of the field, which is alive today and tomorrow is thrown into the furnace, will He not much more clothe you? You of little faith!

31 Do not worry then, saying, 'What will we eat?' or 'What will we drink?' or 'What will we wear for clothing?'

32 For the Gentiles eagerly seek all these things; for your heavenly Father knows that you need all these things.

33 But seek first His kingdom and His righteousness, and all these things will be added to you.

34 So do not worry about tomorrow; for tomorrow will care for itself. Each day has enough trouble of its own."

MATTHEW 18

15 "If your brother sins, go and show him his fault in private; if he listens to you, you have won your brother.

16 But if he does not listen to you, take one or two more with you, so that BY THE MOUTH OF TWO OR THREE WITNESSES EVERY FACT MAY BE CONFIRMED.

17 If he refuses to listen to them, tell it to the church; and if he refuses to listen even to the church, let him be to you as a Gentile and a tax collector.

18 Truly I say to you, whatever you bind on earth shall have been bound in heaven; and whatever you loose on earth shall have been loosed in heaven.

19 Again I say to you, that if two of you agree on earth about anything that they may ask, it shall be done for them by My Father who is in heaven.

20 For where two or three have gathered together in My name, I am there in their midst."

MATTHEW 18

21 Peter came and said to [Jesus], "Lord, how often shall my brother sin against me and I forgive him? Up to seven times?"

22 Jesus said to him, "I do not say to you, up to seven times, but up to seventy times seven.

23 For this reason the kingdom of heaven may be compared to a king who wished to settle accounts with his slaves.

24 When he had begun to settle them, one who owed him ten thousand talents was brought to him.

25 But since he did not have the means to repay, his lord commanded him to be sold, along with his wife and children and all that he had, and repayment to be made.

26 So the slave fell to the ground and prostrated himself before him, saying, 'Have patience with me and I will repay you everything.'

27 And the lord of that slave felt compassion and released him and forgave him the debt.

28 But that slave went out and found one of his fellow slaves who owed him a hundred denarii; and he seized him and began to choke him, saying, 'Pay back what you owe.'

29 So his fellow slave fell to the ground and began to plead with him, saying, 'Have patience with me and I will repay you.'

30 But he was unwilling and went and threw him in prison until he should pay back what was owed.

31 So when his fellow slaves saw what had happened, they were deeply grieved and came and reported to their lord all that had happened.

32 Then summoning him, his lord said to him, 'You wicked slave, I forgave you all that debt because you pleaded with me.

33 'Should you not also have had mercy on your fellow slave, in the same way that I had mercy on you?'

34 And his lord, moved with anger, handed him over to the torturers until he should repay all that was owed him.

35 My heavenly Father will also do the same to you, if each of you does not forgive his brother from your heart."

MATTHEW 23

5 "[The scribes and the Pharisees] do all their deeds to be noticed by men; for they broaden their phylacteries and lengthen the tassels of their garments.

6 They love the place of honor at banquets and the chief seats in the synagogues,

7 and respectful greetings in the market places, and being called Rabbi by men. . . .

13 "But woe to you, scribes and Pharisees, hypocrites, because you shut off the kingdom of heaven from people; for you do not enter in yourselves, nor do you allow those who are entering to go in.

14 Woe to you, scribes and Pharisees, hypocrites, because you devour widows' houses, and for a pretense you make long prayers; therefore you will receive greater condemnation.

15 "Woe to you, scribes and Pharisees, hypocrites, because you travel around on sea and land to make one proselyte; and when he becomes one, you make him twice as much a son of hell as yourselves. . . .

23 "Woe to you, scribes and Pharisees, hypocrites! For you tithe mint and dill and cummin, and have neglected the weightier provisions of the law: justice and mercy and faithfulness; but these are the things you should have done without neglecting the others. . . .

25 "Woe to you, scribes and Pharisees, hypocrites! For you clean the outside of the cup and of the dish, but inside they are full of robbery and self-indulgence. . . .

27 "Woe to you, scribes and Pharisees, hypocrites! For you are like whitewashed tombs which on the outside appear beautiful, but inside they are full of dead men's bones and all uncleanness. . . .

29 "Woe to you, scribes and Pharisees, hypocrites! For you build the tombs of the prophets and adorn the monuments of the righteous."

MATTHEW 25

34 "The King will say to those on His right, 'Come, you who are blessed of My Father, inherit the kingdom prepared for you from the foundation of the world.

35 For I was hungry, and you gave Me something to eat; I was thirsty, and you gave Me something to drink; I was a stranger, and you invited Me in;

36 naked, and you clothed Me; I was sick, and you visited Me; I was in prison, and you came to me.'

37 Then the righteous will answer Him, 'Lord, when did we see You hungry, and feed You, or thirsty, and give You something to drink?

38 And when did we see you a stranger, and invite You in, or naked, and clothe You?

39 When did we see You sick, or in prison, and come to You?'

40 The King will answer and say to them, 'Truly I say to you, to the extent that you did it to one of

these brothers of Mine, even the least of them, you did it to Me.' ”

LUKE 4

1 Jesus, full of the Holy Spirit, returned from the Jordan and was led around by the Spirit in the wilderness

2 for forty days, being tempted by the devil. And He ate nothing during those days, and when they had ended, he became hungry.

3 And the devil said to Him, “If You are the Son of God, tell this stone to become bread.”

4 And Jesus answered him, “It is written, ‘MAN SHALL NOT LIVE ON BREAD ALONE.’ ”

5 And he led Him up and showed Him all the kingdoms of the world in a moment of time.

6 And the devil said to Him, “I will give You all this domain and its glory; for it has been handed over to me, and I give it to whomever I wish.

7 Therefore if You worship before me, it shall all be Yours.”

8 Jesus answered him, “It is written, ‘YOU SHALL WORSHIP THE LORD YOUR GOD AND SERVE HIM ONLY.’ ”

9 And he led Him to Jerusalem and had Him stand on the pinnacle of the temple, and said to Him, “If You are the Son of God, throw Yourself down from here;

10 for it is written, ‘HE WILL COMMAND HIS ANGELS CONCERNING YOU TO GUARD YOU,’

11 and, ‘ON THEIR HANDS THEY WILL BEAR YOU UP, SO THAT YOU WILL NOT STRIKE YOUR FOOT AGAINST A STONE.’ ”

12 And Jesus answered and said to him, “It is said, ‘YOU SHALL NOT PUT THE LORD YOUR GOD TO THE TEST.’ ”

13 When the devil had finished every temptation, he left Him until an opportune time.

LUKE 6

43 “There is no good tree which produces bad fruit, nor, on the other hand, a bad tree which produces good fruit.

44 For each tree is known by its own fruit. For men do not gather figs from thorns, nor do they pick grapes from a briar bush.

45 The good man out of the good treasure of his heart brings forth what is good; and the evil man out of the evil treasure brings forth what is evil; for his mouth speaks from that which fills his heart.

46 Why do you call Me, ‘Lord, Lord,’ and do not do what I say?

47 Everyone who comes to Me and hears My words and acts on them, I will show you whom he is like:

48 he is like a man building a house, who dug deep and laid a foundation on the rock; and when a flood occurred, the torrent burst against that house and could not shake it, because it had been well built.

49 But the one who has heard and has not acted accordingly, is like a man who built a house on the ground without any foundation; and the torrent burst against it and immediately it collapsed, and the ruin of that house was great.”

LUKE 10

30 Jesus replied and said, “A man was going down from Jerusalem to Jericho, and fell among robbers, and they stripped him and beat him, and went away leaving him half dead.

31 And by chance a priest was going down on that road, and when he saw him, he passed by on the other side.

32 Likewise a Levite also, when he came to the place and saw him, passed by on the other side.

33 But a Samaritan, who was on a journey, came upon him; and when he saw him, he felt compassion,

34 and came to him and bandaged up his wounds, pouring oil and wine on them; and he put him on his own beast, and brought him to an inn and took care of him.

35 On the next day he took out two denarii and gave them to the innkeeper and said, ‘Take care of him; and whatever more you spend, when I return I will repay you.’

36 Which of these three do you think proved to be a neighbor to the man who fell into the robbers' hands?”

37 And he said, “The one who showed mercy toward him.” Then Jesus said to him, “Go and do the same.”

LUKE 16

19 “Now there was a rich man, and he habitually dressed in purple and fine linen, joyously living in splendor every day.

20 And a poor man named Lazarus was laid at his gate, covered with sores,

21 and longing to be fed with the crumbs which were falling from the rich man's table; besides, even the dogs were coming and licking his sores.

22 Now the poor man died and was carried

away by the angels to Abraham's bosom; and the rich man also died and was buried.

23 In Hades he lifted up his eyes, being in torment, and saw Abraham far away and Lazarus in his bosom.

24 And he cried out and said, 'Father Abraham, have mercy on me, and send Lazarus so that he may dip the tip of his finger in water and cool off my tongue, for I am in agony in this flame.'

25 But Abraham said, 'Child, remember that during your life you received your good things, and likewise Lazarus bad things; but now he is being comforted here, and you are in agony.

26 And besides all this, between us and you there is a great chasm fixed, so that those who wish to come over from here to you will not be able, and that none may cross over from there to us.'

27 And he said, 'Then I beg you, father, that you send him to my father's house

28 for I have five brothers—in order that he may warn them, so that they will not also come to this place of torment.'

29 But Abraham said, 'They have Moses and the Prophets; let them hear them.'

30 But he said, 'No, father Abraham, but if someone goes to them from the dead, they will repent!'

31 But he said to him, 'If they do not listen to Moses and the Prophets, they will not be persuaded even if someone rises from the dead.' "

ROMANS 3

10 As it is written, "THERE IS NONE RIGHTEOUS, NOT EVEN ONE;

11 THERE IS NONE WHO UNDERSTANDS, THERE IS NONE WHO SEEKS FOR GOD;

12 ALL HAVE TURNED ASIDE, TOGETHER THEY HAVE BECOME USELESS; THERE IS NONE WHO DOES GOOD, THERE IS NOT EVEN ONE."

13 "THEIR THROAT IS AN OPEN GRAVE, WITH THEIR TONGUES THEY KEEP DECEIVING," "THE POISON OF ASPS IS UNDER THEIR LIPS";

14 "WHOSE MOUTH IS FULL OF CURSING AND BITTERNESS";

15 "THEIR FEET ARE SWIFT TO SHED BLOOD,

16 DESTRUCTION AND MISERY ARE IN THEIR PATHS,

17 AND THE PATH OF PEACE THEY HAVE NOT KNOWN."

18 "THERE IS NO FEAR OF GOD BEFORE THEIR EYES."

1 CORINTHIANS 5

1 It is actually reported that there is immorality among you, and immorality of such a kind as does not exist even among the Gentiles, that someone has his father's wife.

2 You have become arrogant and have not mourned instead, so that the one who had done this deed would be removed from your midst.

3 For I, on my part, though absent in body but present in spirit, have already judged him who has so committed this, as though I were present.

4 In the name of our Lord Jesus, when you are assembled, and I with you in spirit, with the power of our Lord Jesus,

5 I have decided to deliver such a one to Satan for the destruction of his flesh, so that his spirit may be saved in the day of the Lord Jesus.

6 Your boasting is not good. Do you not know that a little leaven leavens the whole lump of dough?

7 Clean out the old leaven so that you may be a new lump, just as you are in fact unleavened. For Christ our Passover also has been sacrificed.

8 Therefore let us celebrate the feast, not with old leaven, nor with the leaven of malice and wickedness, but with the unleavened bread of sincerity and truth.

9 I wrote you in my letter not to associate with immoral people;

10 I did not at all mean with the immoral people of this world, or with the covetous and swindlers, or with idolaters, for then you would have to go out of the world.

11 But actually, I wrote to you not to associate with any so-called brother if he is an immoral person, or covetous, or an idolater, or a reviler, or a drunkard, or a swindler—not even to eat with such a one.

12 For what have I to do with judging outsiders? Do you not judge those who are within the church?

13 But those who are outside, God judges. REMOVE THE WICKED MAN FROM AMONG YOURSELVES.

2 CORINTHIANS 6

1 Working together with [God], we also urge you not to receive the grace of God in vain . . .

3 giving no cause for offense in anything, so that the ministry will not be discredited,

4 but in everything commending ourselves as servants of God, in much endurance, in afflictions, in hardships, in distresses,

5 in beatings, in imprisonments, in tumults, in labors, in sleeplessness, in hunger,

6 in purity, in knowledge, in patience, in kindness, in the Holy Spirit, in genuine love,

7 in the word of truth, in the power of God; by the weapons of righteousness for the right hand and the left,

8 by glory and dishonor, by evil report and good report; regarded as deceivers and yet true;

9 as unknown yet well-known, as dying yet behold, we live; as punished yet not put to death,

10 as sorrowful yet always rejoicing, as poor yet making many rich, as having nothing yet possessing all things.

2 CORINTHIANS 11

23 Are they servants of Christ?—I speak as if insane—I more so; in far more labors, in far more imprisonments, beaten times without number, often in danger of death.

24 Five times I received from the Jews thirty-nine lashes.

25 Three times I was beaten with rods, once I was stoned, three times I was shipwrecked, a night and a day I have spent in the deep.

26 I have been on frequent journeys, in dangers from rivers, dangers from robbers, dangers from my countrymen, dangers from the Gentiles, dangers in the city, dangers in the wilderness, dangers on the sea, dangers among false brethren;

27 I have been in labor and hardship, through many sleepless nights, in hunger and thirst, often without food, in cold and exposure.

28 Apart from such external things, there is the daily pressure on me of concern for all the churches.

29 Who is weak without my being weak? Who is led into sin without my intense concern?

30 If I have to boast, I will boast of what pertains to my weakness.

31 The God and Father of the Lord Jesus, He who is blessed forever, knows that I am not lying.

32 In Damascus the ethnarch under Aretas the king was guarding the city of the Damascenes in order to seize me,

33 and I was let down in a basket through a window in the wall, and so escaped his hands.

GALATIANS 5

16 I say, walk by the Spirit, and you will not carry out the desire of the flesh.

17 For the flesh sets its desire against the Spirit, and the Spirit against the flesh; for these are in opposition to one another, so that you may not do the things that you please.

18 But if you are led by the Spirit, you are not under the Law.

19 Now the deeds of the flesh are evident, which are: immorality, impurity, sensuality,

20 idolatry, sorcery, enmities, strife, jealousy, outbursts of anger, disputes, dissensions, factions,

21 envying, drunkenness, carousing, and things like these, of which I forewarn you, just as I have forewarned you, that those who practice such things will not inherit the kingdom of God.

22 But the fruit of the Spirit is love, joy, peace, patience, kindness, goodness, faithfulness,

23 gentleness, self-control; against such things there is no law.

24 Now those who belong to Christ Jesus have crucified the flesh with its passions and desires.

25 If we live by the Spirit, let us also walk by the Spirit.

26 Let us not become boastful, challenging one another, envying one another.

EPHESIANS 5

22 Wives, be subject to your own husbands, as to the Lord.

23 For the husband is the head of the wife, as Christ also is the head of the church, He Himself being the Savior of the body.

24 But as the church is subject to Christ, so also the wives ought to be to their husbands in everything.

25 Husbands, love your wives, just as Christ also loved the church and gave Himself up for her,

26 so that He might sanctify her, having cleansed her by the washing of water with the word,

27 that He might present to Himself the church in all her glory, having no spot or wrinkle or any such thing; but that she would be holy and blameless.

28 So husbands ought also to love their own wives as their own bodies. He who loves his own wife loves himself;

29 for no one ever hated his own flesh, but nourishes and cherishes it, just as Christ also does the church,

30 because we are members of His body.

31 FOR THIS REASON A MAN SHALL LEAVE HIS FATHER AND SHALL BE JOINED TO HIS WIFE, AND THE TWO SHALL BECOME ONE FLESH.

32 This mystery is great; but I am speaking with reference to Christ and the church.

33 Nevertheless, each individual among you also is to love his own wife even as himself, and the wife must see to it that she respects her husband.

1 Now faith is the assurance of things hoped for, the conviction of things not seen.

2 For by it the men of old gained approval.

3 By faith we understand that the worlds were prepared by the word of God, so that what is seen was not made out of things which are visible.

4 By faith Abel offered to God a better sacrifice than Cain, through which he obtained the testimony that he was righteous, God testifying about his gifts, and through faith, though he is dead, he still speaks.

5 By faith Enoch was taken up so that he would not see death; AND HE WAS NOT FOUND BECAUSE GOD TOOK HIM UP; for he obtained the witness that before his being taken up he was pleasing to God.

6 And without faith it is impossible to please Him, for he who comes to God must believe that He is and that He is a rewarder of those who seek Him.

7 By faith Noah, being warned by God about things not yet seen, in reverence prepared an ark for the salvation of his household, by which he condemned the world, and became an heir of the righteousness which is according to faith.

8 By faith Abraham, when he was called, obeyed by going out to a place which he was to receive for an inheritance; and he went out, not knowing where he was going.

9 By faith he lived as an alien in the land of promise, as in a foreign land, dwelling in tents with Isaac and Jacob, fellow heirs of the same promise;

10 for he was looking for the city which has foundations, whose architect and builder is God.

11 By faith even Sarah herself received ability to conceive, even beyond the proper time of life, since she considered Him faithful who had promised.

12 Therefore there was born even of one man, and him as good as dead at that, as many descendants AS THE STARS OF HEAVEN IN NUMBER, AND INNUMERABLE AS THE SAND WHICH IS BY THE SEASHORE.

13 All these died in faith, without receiving the promises, but having seen them and having welcomed them from a distance, and having confessed that they were strangers and exiles on the earth.

14 For those who say such things make it clear that they are seeking a country of their own.

15 And indeed if they had been thinking of that country from which they went out, they would have had opportunity to return.

16 But as it is, they desire a better country, that is, a heavenly one. Therefore God is not ashamed to be called their God; for He has prepared a city for them.

17 By faith Abraham, when he was tested, offered up Isaac, and he who had received the promises was offering up his only begotten son;

18 it was he to whom it was said, "IN ISAAC YOUR DESCENDANTS SHALL BE CALLED."

19 He considered that God is able to raise people even from the dead, from which he also received him back as a type.

20 By faith Isaac blessed Jacob and Esau, even regarding things to come.

21 By faith Jacob, as he was dying, blessed each of the sons of Joseph, and worshiped, leaning on the top of his staff.

22 By faith Joseph, when he was dying, made mention of the exodus of the sons of Israel, and gave orders concerning his bones.

23 By faith Moses, when he was born, was hidden for three months by his parents, because they saw he was a beautiful child; and they were not afraid of the king's edict.

24 By faith Moses, when he had grown up, refused to be called the son of Pharaoh's daughter,

25 choosing rather to endure ill-treatment with the people of God than to enjoy the passing pleasures of sin,

26 considering the reproach of Christ greater riches than the treasures of Egypt; for he was looking to the reward.

27 By faith he left Egypt, not fearing the wrath of the king; for he endured, as seeing Him who is unseen.

28 By faith he kept the Passover and the sprinkling of the blood, so that he who destroyed the firstborn would not touch them.

29 By faith they passed through the Red Sea as though they were passing through dry land; and the Egyptians, when they attempted it, were drowned.

30 By faith the walls of Jericho fell down after they had been encircled for seven days.

31 By faith Rahab the harlot did not perish along with those who were disobedient, after she had welcomed the spies in peace.

32 And what more shall I say? For time will fail me if I tell of Gideon, Barak, Samson, Jephthah, of David and Samuel and the prophets,

33 who by faith conquered kingdoms, performed acts of righteousness, obtained promises, shut the mouths of lions,

34 quenched the power of fire, escaped the edge of the sword, from weakness were made strong, became mighty in war, put foreign armies to flight.

35 Women received back their dead by resurrection; and others were tortured, not accepting their release, so that they might obtain a better resurrection;

36 and others experienced mockings and scourgings, yes, also chains and imprisonment.

37 They were stoned, they were sawn in two, they were tempted, they were put to death with the sword; they went about in sheepskins, in goatskins, being destitute, afflicted, ill-treated

38 (men of whom the world was not worthy), wandering in deserts and mountains and caves and holes in the ground.

39 And all these, having gained approval through their faith, did not receive what was promised,

40 because God had provided something better for us, so that apart from us they would not be made perfect.

JAMES

1:1 James, a bond-servant of God and of the Lord Jesus Christ, To the twelve tribes who are dispersed abroad: Greetings.

1:2 Consider it all joy, my brethren, when you encounter various trials,

1:3 knowing that the testing of your faith produces endurance.

1:4 And let endurance have its perfect result, so that you may be perfect and complete, lacking in nothing.

1:5 But if any of you lacks wisdom, let him ask of God, who gives to all generously and without reproach, and it will be given to him.

1:6 But he must ask in faith without any doubting, for the one who doubts is like the surf of the sea, driven and tossed by the wind.

1:7 For that man ought not to expect that he will receive anything from the Lord,

1:8 being a double-minded man, unstable in all his ways.

1:9 But the brother of humble circumstances is to glory in his high position;

1:10 and the rich man is to glory in his humiliation, because like flowering grass he will pass away.

1:11 For the sun rises with a scorching wind and withers the grass; and its flower falls off and the beauty of its appearance is destroyed; so too the rich man in the midst of his pursuits will fade away.

1:12 Blessed is a man who perseveres under trial; for once he has been approved, he will receive the crown of life which the Lord has promised to those who love Him.

1:13 Let no one say when he is tempted, "I am being tempted by God"; for God cannot be tempted by evil, and He Himself does not tempt anyone.

1:14 But each one is tempted when he is carried away and enticed by his own lust.

1:15 Then when lust has conceived, it gives birth to sin; and when sin is accomplished, it brings forth death.

1:16 Do not be deceived, my beloved brethren.

1:17 Every good thing given and every perfect gift is from above, coming down from the Father of lights, with whom there is no variation or shifting shadow.

1:18 In the exercise of His will He brought us forth by the word of truth, so that we would be a kind of first fruits among His creatures.

1:19 This you know, my beloved brethren. But everyone must be quick to hear, slow to speak and slow to anger;

1:20 for the anger of man does not achieve the righteousness of God.

1:21 Therefore, putting aside all filthiness and all that remains of wickedness, in humility receive the word implanted, which is able to save your souls.

1:22 But prove yourselves doers of the word, and not merely hearers who delude themselves.

1:23 For if anyone is a hearer of the word and not a doer, he is like a man who looks at his natural face in a mirror;

1:24 for once he has looked at himself and gone away, he has immediately forgotten what kind of person he was.

1:25 But one who looks intently at the perfect law, the law of liberty, and abides by it, not having become a forgetful hearer but an effectual doer, this man will be blessed in what he does.

1:26 If anyone thinks himself to be religious, and yet does not bridle his tongue but deceives his own heart, this man's religion is worthless.

1:27 Pure and undefiled religion in the sight of our God and Father is this: to visit orphans and widows in their distress, and to keep oneself unstained by the world.

2:1 My brethren, do not hold your faith in our glorious Lord Jesus Christ with an attitude of personal favoritism.

2:2 For if a man comes into your assembly with a gold ring and dressed in fine clothes, and there also comes in a poor man in dirty clothes,

2:3 and you pay special attention to the one who is wearing the fine clothes, and say, "You sit here in a good place," and you say to the poor man, "You stand over there, or sit down by my footstool,"

2:4 have you not made distinctions among yourselves, and become judges with evil motives?

2:5 Listen, my beloved brethren: did not God choose the poor of this world to be rich in faith and heirs of the kingdom which He promised to those who love Him?

2:6 But you have dishonored the poor man. Is it not the rich who oppress you and personally drag you into court?

2:7 Do they not blaspheme the fair name by which you have been called?

2:8 If, however, you are fulfilling the royal law according to the Scripture, "YOU SHALL LOVE YOUR NEIGHBOR AS YOURSELF," you are doing well.

2:9 But if you show partiality, you are committing sin and are convicted by the law as transgressors.

2:10 For whoever keeps the whole law and yet stumbles in one point, he has become guilty of all.

2:11 For He who said, "DO NOT COMMIT ADULTERY," also said, "DO NOT COMMIT MURDER." Now if you do not commit adultery, but do commit murder, you have become a transgressor of the law.

2:12 So speak and so act as those who are to be judged by the law of liberty.

2:13 For judgment will be merciless to one who has shown no mercy; mercy triumphs over judgment.

2:14 What use is it, my brethren, if someone says he has faith but he has no works? Can that faith save him?

2:15 If a brother or sister is without clothing and in need of daily food,

2:16 and one of you says to them, "Go in peace, be warmed and be filled," and yet you do not give them what is necessary for their body, what use is that?

2:17 Even so faith, if it has no works, is dead, being by itself.

2:18 But someone may well say, "You have faith and I have works; show me your faith without the works, and I will show you my faith by my works."

2:19 You believe that God is one. You do well; the demons also believe, and shudder.

2:20 But are you willing to recognize, you foolish fellow, that faith without works is useless?

2:21 Was not Abraham our father justified by works when he offered up Isaac his son on the altar?

2:22 You see that faith was working with his works, and as a result of the works, faith was perfected;

2:23 and the Scripture was fulfilled which says, "AND ABRAHAM BELIEVED GOD, AND IT WAS RECKONED TO HIM AS RIGHTEOUSNESS," and he was called the friend of God.

2:24 You see that a man is justified by works and not by faith alone.

2:25 In the same way, was not Rahab the harlot also justified by works when she received the messengers and sent them out by another way?

2:26 For just as the body without the spirit is dead, so also faith without works is dead.

3:1 Let not many of you become teachers, my brethren, knowing that as such we will incur a stricter judgment.

3:2 For we all stumble in many ways. If anyone does not stumble in what he says, he is a perfect man, able to bridle the whole body as well.

3:3 Now if we put the bits into the horses' mouths so that they will obey us, we direct their entire body as well.

3:4 Look at the ships also, though they are so great and are driven by strong winds, are still directed by a very small rudder wherever the inclination of the pilot desires.

3:5 So also the tongue is a small part of the body, and yet it boasts of great things. See how great a forest is set aflame by such a small fire!

3:6 And the tongue is a fire, the very world of iniquity; the tongue is set among our members as that which defiles the entire body, and sets on fire the course of our life, and is set on fire by hell.

3:7 For every species of beasts and birds, of reptiles and creatures of the sea, is tamed and has been tamed by the human race.

3:8 But no one can tame the tongue; it is a restless evil and full of deadly poison.

3:9 With it we bless our Lord and Father, and with it we curse men, who have been made in the likeness of God;

3:10 from the same mouth come both blessing and cursing. My brethren, these things ought not to be this way.

3:11 Does a fountain send out from the same opening both fresh and bitter water?

3:12 Can a fig tree, my brethren, produce olives,

or a vine produce figs? Nor can salt water produce fresh.

3:13 Who among you is wise and understanding? Let him show by his good behavior his deeds in the gentleness of wisdom.

3:14 But if you have bitter jealousy and selfish ambition in your heart, do not be arrogant and so lie against the truth.

3:15 This wisdom is not that which comes down from above, but is earthly, natural, demonic.

3:16 For where jealousy and selfish ambition exist, there is disorder and every evil thing.

3:17 But the wisdom from above is first pure, then peaceable, gentle, reasonable, full of mercy and good fruits, unwavering, without hypocrisy.

3:18 And the seed whose fruit is righteousness is sown in peace by those who make peace.

4:1 What is the source of quarrels and conflicts among you? Is not the source your pleasures that wage war in your members?

4:2 You lust and do not have; so you commit murder. You are envious and cannot obtain; so you fight and quarrel. You do not have because you do not ask.

4:3 You ask and do not receive, because you ask with wrong motives, so that you may spend it on your pleasures.

4:4 You adulteresses, do you not know that friendship with the world is hostility toward God? Therefore whoever wishes to be a friend of the world makes himself an enemy of God.

4:5 Or do you think that the Scripture speaks to no purpose: "He jealously desires the Spirit which He has made to dwell in us"?

4:6 But He gives a greater grace. Therefore it says, "GOD IS OPPOSED TO THE PROUD, BUT GIVES GRACE TO THE HUMBLE."

4:7 Submit therefore to God. Resist the devil and he will flee from you.

4:8 Draw near to God and He will draw near to you. Cleanse your hands, you sinners; and purify your hearts, you double-minded.

4:9 Be miserable and mourn and weep; let your laughter be turned into mourning and your joy to gloom.

4:10 Humble yourselves in the presence of the Lord, and He will exalt you.

4:11 Do not speak against one another, brethren. He who speaks against a brother or judges his brother, speaks against the law and judges the law; but if you judge the law, you are not a doer of the law but a judge of it.

4:12 There is only one Lawgiver and Judge, the One who is able to save and to destroy; but who are you who judge your neighbor?

4:13 Come now, you who say, "Today or tomorrow we will go to such and such a city, and spend a year there and engage in business and make a profit."

4:14 Yet you do not know what your life will be like tomorrow. You are just a vapor that appears for a little while and then vanishes away.

4:15 Instead, you ought to say, "If the Lord wills, we will live and also do this or that."

4:16 But as it is, you boast in your arrogance; all such boasting is evil.

4:17 Therefore, to one who knows the right thing to do and does not do it, to him it is sin.

5:1 Come now, you rich, weep and howl for your miseries which are coming upon you.

5:2 Your riches have rotted and your garments have become moth-eaten.

5:3 Your gold and your silver have rusted; and their rust will be a witness against you and will consume your flesh like fire. It is in the last days that you have stored up your treasure!

5:4 Behold, the pay of the laborers who mowed your fields, and which has been withheld by you, cries out against you; and the outcry of those who did the harvesting has reached the ears of the Lord of Sabaoth.

5:5 You have lived luxuriously on the earth and led a life of wanton pleasure; you have fattened your hearts in a day of slaughter.

5:6 You have condemned and put to death the righteous man; he does not resist you.

5:7 Therefore be patient, brethren, until the coming of the Lord. The farmer waits for the precious produce of the soil, being patient about it, until it gets the early and late rains.

5:8 You too be patient; strengthen your hearts, for the coming of the Lord is near.

5:9 Do not complain, brethren, against one another, so that you yourselves may not be judged; behold, the Judge is standing right at the door.

5:10 As an example, brethren, of suffering and patience, take the prophets who spoke in the name of the Lord.

5:11 We count those blessed who endured. You have heard of the endurance of Job and have seen the outcome of the Lord's dealings, that the Lord is full of compassion and is merciful.

5:12 But above all, my brethren, do not swear, either by heaven or by earth or with any other oath; but your yes is to be yes, and your no, no, so that you may not fall under judgment.

5:13 Is anyone among you suffering? Then he must pray. Is anyone cheerful? He is to sing praises.

5:14 Is anyone among you sick? Then he must call for the elders of the church and they are to pray over him, anointing him with oil in the name of the Lord;

5:15 and the prayer offered in faith will restore the one who is sick, and the Lord will raise him up, and if he has committed sins, they will be forgiven him.

5:16 Therefore, confess your sins to one another, and pray for one another so that you may be healed. The effective prayer of a righteous man can accomplish much.

5:17 Elijah was a man with a nature like ours, and he prayed earnestly that it would not rain, and it did not rain on the earth for three years and six months.

5:18 Then he prayed again, and the sky poured rain and the earth produced its fruit.

5:19 My brethren, if any among you strays from the truth and one turns him back,

5:20 let him know that he who turns a sinner from the error of his way will save his soul from death and will cover a multitude of sins.

1 Peter 4

12 Beloved, do not be surprised at the fiery ordeal among you, which comes upon you for your testing, as though some strange thing were happening to you;

13 but to the degree that you share the sufferings of Christ, keep on rejoicing, so that also at the revelation of His glory you may rejoice with exultation.

14 If you are reviled for the name of Christ, you are blessed, because the Spirit of glory and of God rests on you.

15 Make sure that none of you suffers as a murderer, or thief, or evildoer, or a troublesome meddler;

16 but if anyone suffers as a Christian, he is not to be ashamed, but is to glorify God in this name.

17 For it is time for judgment to begin with the household of God; and if it begins with us first, what will be the outcome for those who do not obey the gospel of God?

18 AND IF IT IS WITH DIFFICULTY THAT THE RIGHTEOUS IS SAVED, WHAT WILL BECOME OF THE GODLESS MAN AND THE SINNER?

19 Therefore, those also who suffer according to the will of God shall entrust their souls to a faithful Creator in doing what is right.

Revelation 20

11 I saw a great white throne and Him who sat upon it, from whose presence earth and heaven fled away, and no place was found for them.

12 And I saw the dead, the great and the small, standing before the throne, and books were opened; and another book was opened, which is the book of life; and the dead were judged from the things which were written in the books, according to their deeds.

13 And the sea gave up the dead which were in it, and death and Hades gave up the dead which were in them; and they were judged, every one of them according to their deeds.

14 Then death and Hades were thrown into the lake of fire. This is the second death, the lake of fire.

15 And if anyone's name was not found written in the book of life, he was thrown into the lake of fire.

APPENDIX B—
GOD'S PLAN OF SALVATION

In America today, most people either do not know what it means to be saved or do not understand that salvation is something they urgently need. God's plan of salvation is good news only when we understand the really bad news; namely, that all of us have broken God's law and the consequences are eternally serious.[223] As a result of Adam and Eve's rebellion, something happened not just "to" them but "in" them that continues to have a residual effect on us— their descendants. It is as if Adam acquired bad blood that was passed to all generations. Our inherited sin nature places each of us at odds with a pure and holy God.

Without a *spiritual transfusion,* our condition will end in eternal death (hell).[224] Within the context of this bad news, the tremendous good news of the gospel is fully realized. Through the cleansing power of the blood of Jesus Christ, God has made a way of escape.

Because Jesus was God the Son, His death on the cross satisfied—made propitiation for—the sin debt for all people.[225] This means that the ransom price for your sentence of eternal death has already been deposited by Christ into your account.[226] Whatever amount you need to be reconciled to God is available to you through His Son—and through Him alone.[227] When you come to Jesus, He will require one thing—that you yield your life to be spiritually born anew in Him.[228] So how does one go about being born anew?

1. BEGIN WITH AN HONEST AND SINCERE HEART

God knows exactly where you are and what you think and feel about Him. Therefore, you're free to—indeed you must—tell Him the truth. If you're not sure God exists, tell Him. Then ask Him to reveal Himself to you that you may fully believe in Him. If you don't like reading His Word or you think His principles are too demanding or you don't

[223] **ROMANS 3; 6**
3:23 For all have sinned and fall short of the glory of God.
6:23 For the wages of sin is death, but the free gift of God is eternal life.

[224] **ROMANS 5**
12 Therefore, just as through one man sin entered into the world, and death through sin, and so death spread to all men, because all sinned.

[225] **1 JOHN 2**
2 And He Himself is the propitiation for our sins; and not for ours only, but also for those of the whole world.

[226] **ROMANS 3**
24-26 [We are] justified as a gift by His grace through the redemption which is in Christ Jesus; whom God displayed publicly as a propitiation in His blood through faith . . . in the forbearance of God He passed over the sins previously committed; . . . that He would be just and the justifier of the one who has faith in Jesus.

[227] **ACTS 4**
12 There is salvation in no one else; for there is no other name [besides Jesus] under heaven that has been given among men, by which we must be saved.

[228] 1 PETER 3

18 For Christ also died for sins once for all, the just for the unjust . . . having been put to death in the flesh, but made alive in the spirit.

[229] 1 PETER 2

2 Like newborn babies, long for the pure milk of the word, so that by it you may grow in respect to salvation.

[230] ROMANS 3

10-12 As it is written, "THERE IS NONE RIGHTEOUS, NOT EVEN ONE; THERE IS NONE WHO UNDER-STANDS, THERE IS NONE WHO SEEKS FOR GOD; ALL HAVE TURNED ASIDE, TOGETHER THEY HAVE BECOME USE-LESS; THERE IS NONE WHO DOES GOOD, THERE IS NOT EVEN ONE."

[231] 1 JOHN 1

9 If we confess our sins, He is faithful and righteous to forgive us our sins and to cleanse us from all unrighteousness.

[232] 2 CORINTHIANS 7

10 For the sorrow that is according to the will of God pro-duces a repentance without regret, leading to salvation, but the sorrow of the world pro-duces death.

[233] EPHESIANS 2

8-9 For by grace you have been saved through faith; and that not of yourselves, it is the gift of God; not as a result of works, so that no one may boast.

like going to church, tell Him. Ask Him to help you through your resistance and to create a desire to know Him through His Word and through His people.[229] Whatever it is that has kept you from coming to God—pride, fear, shame, guilt, anger, disappointment, unbelief, lack of knowledge—tell Him about it and ask Him to bring you to a place of acceptance of His will in your life.

2. CONFESS YOUR SIN AND ASK GOD'S FORGIVENESS

See yourself among the all who have sinned.[223] Don't get sidetracked by focusing on your good points or by compar-ing yourself favorably to others—even to Christians. Don't confuse religious habits, such as church attendance or Christian service, with evidence of your own goodness. When measured against a pure and holy God, all human righteousness is worthless. Agree with God's Word that you are a sinner, and acknowledge your failed efforts at being good.[230] Confess the specific sins you are aware of, such as pride, jealousy, prejudice, intellectualism, anger, rebellion, or anything you see in your life that is unlike Christ.[231] Ask God to make you aware of any hidden sins and convict you of sin until you are truly and deeply sorry for displeasing Him.[232]

3. RECOGNIZE THAT YOU CANNOT SAVE YOURSELF

Understand that you need Someone to do in you what you cannot do in and for yourself.[233] You cannot save yourself, call yourself to God, change yourself, or even really believe in God by your own efforts.[234] In fact, you can't even desire to come to God by your own intent.[235] But this is great news. It means that any flicker of interest you have toward knowing God is evidence that He is calling you personally to Himself. Your part is to respond to His calling and to yield to His rule and reign in your life. You can trust Him, for He is interested only in your highest good.

4. WATCH FOR EVIDENCE OF CHANGE FROM THE INSIDE OUT

Don't try to be good. Instead look for changes of the heart—different attitudes, greater love, peace, kindness, joy that spill out in changes in behavior.[236]

Be intentionally introspective—the changes may be subtle at first. Be still before the Lord and allow yourself to sense His presence and His peace. Ask God to let others see changes in you as confirmation that He is at work in your life. If you sense no changes or see no evidence of the Spirit in your life, go back to God and ask Him to reveal anything that may be holding you away from receiving His gift of eternal life. Go through each of these processes again and tell God you will continue seeking Him until He enables you to seek Him with your whole heart that He might be found by you, according to His promise.[237] As you grow in your walk with the Lord, both your awareness of sin and your wonder at the Cross will increase.

Meditate on the Scriptures in the side columns. You may want to pray them back to God as your own words, from your heart. Be assured. He is waiting and He will answer you.

Note: When you pray to receive Christ, seek out a Bible-believing church for fellowship, prayer, Bible study, and accountability.

[234]**JOHN 15**
16 "You did not choose Me [Jesus] but I chose you, and appointed you that you would go and bear fruit, and that your fruit would remain."

[235]**JOHN 6**
37,44 "All that the Father gives Me will come to Me, and the one who comes to Me I will certainly not cast out. . . . No one can come to Me unless the Father who sent Me draws him; and I will raise him up on the last day."

[236]**2 CORINTHIANS 5**
17 Therefore if any one is in Christ, he is a new creature; the old things passed away; behold, new things have come.

[237]**1 TIMOTHY 4**
16 Persevere in these things; for as you do this you will ensure salvation both for yourself and for those who hear you.